THE
COPYRIGHT
DILEMMA

Proceedings of a conference held at
Indiana University April 14-15, 1977

Edited by
HERBERT S. WHITE
Professor, Graduate Library School
Indiana University-Bloomington

American Library Association

Chicago 1978

Library of Congress Cataloging in Publication Data

Main entry under title:

The Copyright dilemma.

Sponsored by the Indiana University Graduate Library
School.
1. Copyright--United States--Congresses. I. White,
Herbert S. II. Indiana. University. Graduate
Library School.
KF2994.A2C66   346'.73'0482   78-5929
ISBN 0-8389-0262-6

Printed in the United States of America

C O N T E N T S

iv Contents

PREFACE

The idea for the conference reported in the proceedings which follow grew from the desire to recognize and commemorate the tenth anniversary of the Indiana University Graduate Library School's existence as an independent degree-granting institution. It was decided early to celebrate our birthday party in part in the form of a conference which would permit an interaction of GLS students and faculty with off-campus professionals and experts, provide an opportunity for the return of alumni, and help carry out the School's responsibility toward continuing education for librarians in Indiana and the neighboring regions. It was hoped that such a conference, properly planned and implemented, would attract nationally recognized speakers, and through them a national audience, including many with no direct ties to Indiana University and its Graduate Library School.

The conference proved successful not only in attracting many individuals from the library, education, and publishing communities from Indiana and elsewhere, but also in providing an opportunity for these people to interact with one another, with the experts invited to address the conference, and with faculty and students of the Graduate Library School as well as the Schools of Business, Law, Education, and other professional areas concerned with the use and reproduction of scholarly and research materials.

Both Vice-president Robert O'Neil, senior official of the Bloomington campus, and Dean Bernard M. Fry, Graduate Library School, were active in the planning of this conference from the very outset, and without their ideas, their participation, and their encouragement the conference could never have taken place. In addition, particular thanks must go to the Indiana University Alumni Office, especially to Alumni Secretary Frank Jones, Associate Alumni Secretary Arthur Lotz, and Administrative Assistant Jodi Hollowitz, all of whom grasped early the significance of such a conference for the Graduate Library School and its alumni and were supportive and helpful throughout in both planning and implementation. The Indiana University Conference Bureau, in particular Karen Raleigh and Carol Straub, handled countless details and headed off innumerable crises. Finally, appreciation must be expressed to the students of the Graduate Library School, too numerous to identify individually, who with enthusiasm and high spirits volunteered for the many mundane and thankless tasks, such as handing out registration badges, making plane reservations, and providing chauffeur services, without which no conference can succeed.

Selection of the topic of copyright came naturally, due to the timeliness of the issue and the special relationship which the Indiana University Graduate Library School, and particularly its Research Center for Library and Information Science, has enjoyed with both the library and publishing communities. In the fall of 1976, after many years of debate and several false starts, after lengthy discussions of such informal bodies as the "Upstairs Downstairs" group, and the drawn-out acrimony of the legal suit brought by Williams and Wilkins against the National Library of Medicine, Congress passed the first comprehensive revision of the copyright statute since 1909. The need for new legislation, which the courts in their decisions in Williams and Wilkins clearly pointed out, becomes most obvious when one thinks about the changes in the operation of libraries, the development of networks and consortia, and the improvements in the technology for the reproduction and transmittal of information which have taken place in the last 67 years.

The years since the close of the Johnson administration in 1969 have been kind neither to libraries in

their receipt of support funding, particularly through
federal channels, nor to publishers of scholarly books
and periodicals. Rampant inflationary pressures reflected in the higher costs of labor, paper, and postage, the devaluation of the U.S. dollar, the continued
growth of the scholarly literature, and the ever-
increasing pressure on libraries to provide access to
more and more esoteric materials have all exceeded the
funds available to libraries for materials acquisition.
In the years since 1969 library budgets have grown
slowly if at all and in some instances have actually
decreased.

It is understandable that, in such times of stress,
relationships between publishers and librarians, who
have historically enjoyed excellent rapport, should
come under strain. Studies undertaken for the National
Science Foundation by the Indiana University Graduate
Library School covering the years 1969 to 1973, and
which are now being updated for the years 1974 to 1976,
clearly indicate the increased dependence of publishers
on library purchases, as sales to individual subscribers have shriveled. They also indicate the inabil-
ity of libraries to meet these expectations. The resulting suspicions which have grown around these
stresses, with librarians accusing publishers of wildly
exorbitant price increases to reap obscene profits and
with publishers accusing librarians of sinister con-
spiracies through networks, consortia, and national
data banks to defraud them of their rightful income,
are not surprising. They have been highly emotional,
increasingly vituperative, and generally not based on
fact.

The specific recommendation that our conference deal
with problems of implementation and provisions of the
new copyright law came from Dean Fry. This was endorsed
by the Graduate Library School faculty and enthusiasti-
cally accepted by Vice-president O'Neil. As a prominent
constitutional lawyer with a long-standing interest in
First Amendment rights, Mr. O'Neil could see clearly
the challenges and conflicts of balancing the rights of
the author and publisher as proprietors against those
of the scholar and librarian. The title for the conference, "The Copyright Dilemma - A Rational Outcome,"

came from Dean Fry. It was his feeling, and ours, that the development of a solution through intensive debate and compromise could indeed result in a rational outcome, one with which each of the participating parties might feel reasonably satisfied, one whose implications they understood and appreciated, and one which now required the development of implementing guidelines in the same spirit of cooperation and compromise. The proceedings which follow indicate quite clearly that this assumption was highly premature. There is, as of this writing, no clearly accepted understanding of what the copyright law means in terms of specific application to libraries and copyright owners alike, let alone an agreement on how guidelines are to be developed and implemented. With the implementation virtually upon us, it seems certain that this date will come and pass without any major enlightenment, and that the development of a working relationship will require further negotiation, some trial and error, the probability of litigation, and perhaps some amendatory legislation.

In planning this conference on copyright we were aware of the rash of meetings dealing with the new copyright law which had already taken place and which were being planned. We recognized that to be meaningful this conference had to achieve a level of approach not evident in other meetings. The basis for that difference was quickly apparent. Many of the meetings about the copyright law that have been held and continue to be held by interested parties of authors, publishers, and librarians ostensibly are meant to inform; however, they frequently degenerate into one-sided diatribes in which proponents castigate their adversaries for wrongs, real and imagined. It was our intention from the beginning to provide a balanced program of representatives from government, publishers, authors, and secondary information services as well as from the various types of library interests. We planned to allow these individuals adequate time for presentation of their views, for discussion and interchange with one another, and for interaction with members of the audience. We recognized particularly the importance of these informal interchanges and planned from the outset to record and report the entire conference, including comments, questions,

and answers. As the following pages will clearly indicate, some of these interactions were painful for both
speakers and listeners. It is not easy to listen to the
expression of a viewpoint which disagrees with one's
own and far more pleasant to applaud proponents with
whom one concurs.

In selecting a panel of distinguished representatives
for the various viewpoints, we assembled a group of ar-
ticulate experts who, for individual knowledge of their
topics and collective program impression, are not likely
to be matched again. The conference began with a historical overview of copyright legislation, presented by
Professor Maurice Holland of the Indiana University
School of Law. Government representatives included Thomas Brennan, chief counsel of the Senate Subcommittee on
Patents, Trademarks, and Copyright; Jon Baumgarten, general counsel of the Copyright Office at the Library of
Congress; and Robert Frase, assistant executive director
of the Commission on New Technological Uses of Copyrighted Works (CONTU). Also participating were Lee
Burchinal, director of the National Science Foundation's
Division of Science Information, and Alphonse Trezza,
executive director of the National Commission on Libraries and Information Science, who may be considered both
a spokesperson for the government and for the library
profession.

Representatives of the copyright proprietor community
included Irwin Karp, counsel for the Authors League of
America; Bella Linden, senior partner in the law firm
of Linden & Deutsch, which has as its clients a number
of major American publishers; William Koch, director of
publications for the American Institute of Physics; and
Paul Zurkowski, president of the Information Industry
Association.

Representing the library community, in addition to
Mr. Trezza, were Robert Wedgeworth, executive director
of the American Library Association; Richard De Gennaro,
former president of the Association of Research Libraries and director of a major research library; and Efren
Gonzalez, past president and a member of the copyright
committee of the Special Libraries Association.

Vice-president O'Neil, whose contribution was earlier
acknowledged, gave a stimulating and provocative after-

dinner talk on the subject "Intellectual Property and
Intellectual Freedom." If there was any imbalance in
the program, it came inadvertently from the fact that
the proposal for the establishment of a copy payments
center, made by the Association of American Publishers
after the development of the conference program, had
been opposed at that juncture by two of the partici-
pants, both attorneys, Irwin Karp and Bella Linden,
although, since the conference, these differences have
been resolved. Fortunately, the proposal for the center was supported and could therefore be adequately explained by William Koch and Ben Weil, a member of the
audience, who had just been appointed to the post of
coordinator for the implementation of the center. It
is fair, therefore, to comment, as one participant did,
that "All of the players are here." That, of course,
had been our intention and is what, in our judgment,
makes this a significant conference and a significant
set of proceedings.

Now for some final and personal observations. As was
indicated earlier, any assumption that the copyright
debate has had a "rational outcome" is premature at
best. It was disappointing to find, although perhaps
naive to expect anything else, that some of the en-
trenched positions presumably dispensed with by the new
legislation still have adherents. By this I mean that
there are still copyright owners who expect that librarians are prepared to underwrite whatever shortfall other
publication sales provide and some librarians who are
still determined to do as much copying as they can, reasonable or not, if they can get away with it.

It is my own view, as well as that of other representatives of the library community, that implementation
of the new copyright law will have little impact on the
way in which librarians operate and that it will provide
little revenue for authors and publishers from libraries. The development of one or more copy payment centers,
or whatever these centers or clearinghouses will be called, may result from a genuine feeling from some publishers that the revenue they generate will be substantial.
If so, I believe they will be disappointed. On the other
hand, the development of a payment or permission mechan-

ism may have the force of moral suasion and prevent librarians from doing even more copying than they might
otherwise do; it may well be that these centers are
aimed primarily at the education community, in which I
have observed multiple copying has been far more preva-
lent and far more irresponsible than in libraries.

The belief that the implementation of the copyright
law will have little financial impact on libraries and
provide little financial relief to publishers and authors is based on the conclusion that the so-called
copyright compromise represents, in fact, a sweeping
victory for the library community in the wording particularly of Sections 107 and 108 of the new law, when
compared to the initial wordings which emerged from the
Senate report. As Alphonse Trezza stated during his remarks: "The new law is better than the old one." It is
indeed better in my judgment. It is therefore paradoxi-
cal that we find librarians at various library meetings
attacking this "compromise" and publishers defending it.

The belief that the new copyright law will have little impact on libraries stems from the fundamental conclusion, although it is dangerous to summarize a legal
document, that (1) libraries can make, with few limitations, individual copies from journals they already own;
and (2) libraries can borrow up to five times from a
title they do not own. Innumerable studies about collection use, in both large and small libraries, attest
that these two caveats will cover virtually all library
photocopying, with perhaps two exceptions.

One involves the making of multiple copies, usually
for an educator. There is general agreement that such a
practice was as improper under the old law as under the
new, and it is really more of a problem or an accommodation for educators than for librarians. If, as a result,
teachers will be forced to determine whether a title is
actually available before they assign it to be read, such
a restriction can hardly be considered unreasonable.

The second exception concerns the situation in which
the library is in fact borrowing the same title more
than five times in the same year. If this is the case,
then it is probable that the library should be subscribing to such a heavily used title and, if budget
pressures apply, the suspicion still remains that there

may be less frequently used titles which could be cancelled to make room for the more useful ones.

Several speakers referred to the study surveying publisher practices and attitudes concerning authorized journal article copying and licensing carried out for CONTU by the Indiana University Graduate Library School Research Center which distributed and analyzed a CONTU-developed questionnaire. This study has now been completed, and is available from the National Technical Information Service (NTIS) as document PB 271003. To summarize briefly, the findings concerned with publisher attitudes and their expectation of remuneration through some sort of copy payment mechanism indicated that more than half of responding copyrighted journals expected no payment to them from the operation of a copy payment center. It cannot necessarily be inferred that these journals would grant blanket copying permission, but to the extent to which a charge would be placed, it would only serve to cover the operating costs of the payment mechanism or mechanisms. About half of the remaining journals expected a payment to them of no more than 50 cents per transaction. For perhaps 75 percent of the copyrighted journals which responded to the survey it can be assumed, according to initial attitudes, that a payment of $4 or less for copying an article outside the CONTU guidelines would be acceptable. And on analysis of preliminary estimates by librarians, including speakers at the Indiana Copyright Conference, it would appear that charges to individual libraries for such copying would not be substantial.

At the same time, it must also be recognized that there are journal publishers, albeit a smaller number, who expect a more substantial return. About 10 percent of the responding journals indicated a desire to receive more than $4 through any copy authorization mechanism, and it is probable that these represent some of the very special cases of highly expensive, esoteric, and limited circulation journals which both Irwin Karp and Paul Zurkowski mention in their talks. The need for frequent copying outside the CONTU guidelines from these journals could cause serious financial problems for a library.

In summary, this editor believes that the Indiana University conference "The Copyright Dilemma - A Rational

Outcome" makes an important contribution to an understanding of the many conflicting viewpoints concerning
copyright and of the difficulty in resolving them. The
proceedings of the conference are not likely to become
rapidly outdated for these reasons, despite the continuing and rapid changes in library networking and the
establishment of publisher payment centers, and despite
the expected issuance and certain later revision or
amendment of guidelines, or even the development of a
further body of law, through legislation or litigation.

HERBERT S. WHITE

Graduate Library School
Indiana University-Bloomington

Session 1

April 14, 1977

A BRIEF HISTORY OF AMERICAN COPYRIGHT LAW

MAURICE J. HOLLAND

As is true with most facets of American history and especially the history of American law, at least a brief excursion back to the English background is necessary if one is to comprehend what has transpired in the United States. The story in the broad sense begins with the introduction into England of the printing press in the late fifteenth century. Prior to the availability of mechanical printing, there could be no serious problem about putting limitations on reproduction or pirating of works. To the contrary, in the Middle Ages the process of making manuscript books available was so extraordinarily laborious that copying, usually by monks, was commended as a labor of love, and was, for the most part, conducted under the auspices of the church or, at times, noble patrons. There was also a limited degree of literacy. I suppose less than one percent of the population in England at the beginning of the sixteenth century could read. Therefore there was really no possibility of financial rewards to be gained from authorship in anything like the modern sense.

The introduction of the printing press in England coincided with two other larger events, namely the Renaissance and the Reformation, both of which came to England late. The Renaissance changed the attitudes of

Associate Professor, School of Law, Indiana University.

3

European and English society toward literacy, toward
books, and toward learning, and these became rather
fashionable. Up until the Renaissance it was almost
with pride that even the kings of England could boast
they were unable to read. The Reformation contributed
its part, because at least the ability to read scrip-
ture was thought to be necessary for the salvation of
souls. So, throughout the sixteenth and seventeenth
centuries in England there was a considerable increase
in the literate public and the audience or the market
for books. With the press there was the practical possibility of satisfying that market in ways that had
never been true before. There was another thing about
sixteenth- and seventeenth-century England that, indi-
rectly at least, bears on the background of copyright.

The attitude toward printing and publication, although favorable because of the Renaissance and Reformation, in some ways resembles the contemporary attitude
toward plutonium. Both were considered good, perhaps
even necessary, but fraught with the possibilities of
explosive harm to church and state were they to fall into the hands of any but godly and loyal subjects. Therefore the Tudor regime, particularly under Queen Elizabeth, was concerned about controlling what was published
It effected control by a very stringent and efficient
system of licensing. Nothing could be published without
leave of the crown officials appointed for that purpose
What developed was a dual system of licensing. That is,
any individual work to be published had itself to be licensed, usually by a bishop or some other ecclesiastic
if it dealt with religion or by some high government
official if it dealt with politics. Furthermore, each
press had to be licensed. Now this regime of licensing
would have run against the very parsimonious grain of
the Tudor monarchs if they had had to pay out of their
own often meager resources for some corps of secret po-
lice to directly enforce the licensing acts. It was a
characteristic of Tudor ingenuity to engage the self-
interest of private parties to bear that cost and to
carry out the function of enforcement. The private part
most prominently engaged was known as the Stationers
Company, a very august organization and one of the grea
guilds of England.

The Stationers were essentially printers or publishers, to whom the government gave a virtual monopoly in publishing books in England. The number of members varied but was something on the order of twenty, all located in London. The only exceptions, the only presses in England not controlled by the Stationers, were the presses of the universities, which were controlled by ecclesiastics. The Stationers, then, held this monopoly and were, in a sense, part of the establishment. They depended upon the favor of the Crown for their monopoly and could therefore be pretty well depended upon to ensure that no unlicensed works were printed on any of their presses. For reasons of financial self-interest, the Stationers could be depended upon to make sure that no books published other than on their presses could be sold. They were authorized to search out and literally destroy any printed works in England that came to their notice which had not been duly printed on a Stationer's press. This really has only a remote resemblance to copyright as we understand it today. This was censorship, but it carried the seeds of copyright.

The origins of something like copyright must be found not in the broader workings of English law but in the internal regulation that prevailed in the Stationers Company itself. It started in a rather modest way. There were about twenty master printers who worked out a system to decide among themselves who should have the priority for the publication of a given book. The system they devised was straightforward and simple. If a printer acquired a manuscript from an author and intended to print it, he would simply cause the title of that work to be entered on the register of the Stationers Company in the Guildhall in London. Provided no other member of the Stationers Company had previously registered that title, the member making the entry would be recognized, at least among the Stationers, as having the exclusive right of printing and reprinting that book in England for all time, or at least unless matters were changed by a decision among the Stationers themselves. This came to be called by the Stationers "the right of copy" or simply the "copy" in a book.

With the onset of the religious and political controversies of the seventeenth century, which resulted first

in the Glorious Civil War and then the Parliamentary
Revolution, the position of the Stationers and their
monopoly was threatened by increasing demands for an
end to government censorship. Or at least an end to what
we today call "prior censorship," or licensing of the
presses (for many reasons, among them that the censors
often were stupid individuals who couldn't be depended
upon to make sensible judgments even if one grants the
premise of censorship). It was thought that when the
parliamentary forces won the Civil War in 1642 an end
of censorship would occur because the licensing provisions had always been associated with the Crown and now
the Crown was out of power. You'll recall that Milton's
Aeropagitica was really a pamphlet, an elaborate petition to the Long Parliament to abolish what he called
"this noxious system of licensing." However, the degree
of Milton's devotion to the principles of the free press
is often overstated. He simply didn't like licensing because of the stupidity and banality of the censors. He
did not advocate that people should be permitted to publish whatever they pleased. In fact, in the *Aeropagitica*
he said, "Those which otherwise come forth" - that is,
other than from one of the established and permitted
presses - "if they be found mischievous, the fire and
the executioner will be the timeliest and most effectua
remedy that man's prevention can use."

The Long Parliament did not heed Milton's advice and
continued the system of licensing; therefore the Stationers' privileges remained intact. However, all that
changed with the so-called Glorious Revolution of 1688
and the triumph of the Whig Party. For reasons that are
not entirely clear on the historical record, after Jame
II was deposed, Parliament, dominated by the victorious
Whig Party, permitted the Licensing Act, really a serie
of acts accruing over the centuries, to lapse. Thus for
the first time in England one could in a sense set up i
business for one's self, establish a press, and print
without leave either of the Crown or any government officials, and, as well, without regard to the Stationers
monopoly. It is thought that this change reflected the
ideas of such Whig theorists as John Locke. In any even
the difficulty that the Stationers found themselves in
was that, of course, they were permitted to continue wi

their little book of entries and registers and parcel
out the rights of exclusivity among themselves, but
there was no way they could prevent people who were not
members of the Company, the independent presses, from
setting up and going into competition. The Stationers
addressed Parliament in 1709, saying that they were being threatened with bankruptcy because of the prevalence
of piratical presses - printers who were not members of
the Company would wait until a book was published, and
who, if it became popular, would simply pirate it and
recopy it. In any event, despite the tribulations of the
Stationers, and their success with Parliament, censorship was gone from England forever. Thereafter, that is
after about 1695, the libelous, the obscene, the blas-
phemous, and the seditious would be dealt with by judges
in criminal prosecutions rather than by Crown censors
before the event.

Still another change was taking place at the beginning of the eighteenth century, in addition to a
heightened concern for what we would think of as political freedom and freedom of expression: repudiation of
the old mercantilist theory of trade. Under the mercantilist theory of trade it was thought that industry and
trade should be conducted through monopolistic guilds
that were strictly regulated by the government, guilds
like the Stationers Company. The newly emerging forces
of political liberty were also of a mind to establish
more individual economic freedom. Thus property rights,
among them copyright, began to be thought of more as
individual rights than corporate privilege or franchise,
as had been true in the past. Notice that up to this
point, there had been no concern at all for an author's
rights either in the Licensing Acts or in the operations
of the Stationers Company. These were solely for the
benefit of the Crown and of the printers. Authors did
not fare at all well in those days. Occasionally, if
one came along and wrote a book which the powers that
be particularly approved of and wanted to reward, he
would be granted a patent which gave him a perpetual
monopoly for the printing of that book. Such a patent
was a rather valuable subsidy, but those were few and
far between. Other authors not so favored, although many
were well known, even famous, were reduced to petition-

ing Parliament for a license to beg in order to make ends meet.

The rights of authors were inconsequential up to this point. But then came what is always described as the first copyright statute, the Statute of Anne, which was passed by Parliament in 1710. It would be interesting if we knew more about its background. This seemingly sudden decision to favor authors and encourage learning may have arisen because the Whig Party, which was then in power, was in close alliance with a new class of people in England. With growing literacy and other events, it was becoming possible for the first time for a person to aspire to a literary career, an independent professional career as a writer of books. The novel was soon to become important as a literary genre, the short story becoming so considerably later; but up until this time writing (mostly about politics, philosophy, and religion) had usually been done under the auspices of some royal or noble patron. Writers, like other artists, composers and the like, were always dependent on someone. Now it was becoming possible for people like Swift, Dryden, Defoe, Addison, and Steele to function in the way we think of as the modern, independent author. It happened that these men, particularly Addison and Steele, were in close alliance with the Whig Party. In fact Steele was a Whig propagandist. In any event, the year 1710 saw the passage by Parliament of the Statute of Anne which established the main lineaments of modern copyright law, first in England and later in the United States. The basic pattern established by that statute has persisted with amazingly little change, even in this country. That is, amazingly little change occurred until the Copyright Act of 1976, which we are all gathered here today to consider.

The main feature of the Statute of Anne was that it vested copyright in authors, providing a term of protection of 14 years, 14 years for the initial term and 14 years for renewal; the initial term later became 28 years, and in some cases 21 years, both in England and in this country. In fact, it was 21 years for those books that were already printed. For some reason, which I don't pretend to know, copyright terms have always seemed to be in multiples of seven. The protection that

the act afforded vested the exclusive right in the author until and unless he or she assigned the right to
a publisher, which an author would very likely do. A
copyright ran from the date of first publication and
not composition (again a feature of Anglo-American copyright law which has persisted until 1976). This dating
of protection from the date of publication gave rise to
enormous difficulties that have dogged the copyright
law both in England and in this country to the present
day. There were also the rigid formalities of registration and deposit that are familiar to us. Registration
was made in the old Stationers Company Guild Hall as it
always had been, but the privilege of registering was
no longer limited to members of the Company. Anyone who
claimed to be an author, or a publisher by assignment
from an author, could register the title and obtain the
protection of the act. To guard against the possibility
that the Stationers would refuse to register titles for
anyone other than approved members of the Stationers
Company and thereby extend their monopoly, there was a
provision that if the Clerk of the Stationers Company
refused to register a copyright, it could also be secured by a publication of notice of claimed copyright
in the *London Gazette*. There were nine libraries in
England and Scotland that received deposits of a free
copy of every book offered for copyright, a practice
which has remained to the present; in the United States
the Library of Congress is the beneficiary. The remedies for infringement or violation of copyright in the
Statute of Anne are also familiar in that there was a
flat penalty based on each infringing sheet or page
assessed, recoverable in court. It also provided for
destruction of infringing copies.

With the Statute of Anne, I think that perhaps the
time has come to shift to this side of the Atlantic.
If there was any copyright law in colonial America, it
has left no trace. That is not surprising, since we
know less about the law of colonial America than we do
of Anglo-Saxon England. There are some people now working to rectify that situation. It would not be surprising, however, if there were no concern about copyright
in the early colonial days. There were few professional
authors, although certainly newspapers and gazettes and

government documents and the like were published. Most
books as such were almost certainly imported from England. Also, there was no guild structure in colonial
America. Immediately upon the winning of independence,
however, the Continental Congress recommended by resolution that each of the thirteen newly independent
states adopt a copyright statute. The suggested model
was the Statute of Anne. The Continental Congress itself had no power to legislate directly; it could merely exhort the states to legislate on their own behalf.
In fact, each of the states but one did respond with
copyright statutes, all more or less tracking the Statute of Anne. However, these statutes virtually came to
nothing because many of them provided that they did not
become effective until and unless all of the other
states adopted similar provisions. That never quite
came to pass. I believe it was Delaware that never did
enact a copyright statute. Before these interim state
copyright statutes could come into play there was the
Constitutional Convention in Philadelphia, and the matter was then moved to the new federal government.

The men who gathered in Philadelphia in May of 1787
to frame a new constitution, despite their vast differences in many respects, were all men of the Enlightenment who were peculiarly aware of the importance of literature and learning and what they called "science" to
the health and vitality of a new republican form of government. They were also something of cultural national-
ists, and some, Thomas Jefferson and others, were afraid
that such American literature and culture as existed
was far too dependent upon Europe, and on Britain in
particular. Therefore, one of the businesses of the new
national government was to encourage the development of
a new national culture and literature. They included in
the new Constitution, in Article 1, a provision authorizing Congress to promote the progress of science and
the useful arts by securing to writers and inventors
the exclusive rights in their writings and inventions.
This was merely authorization for Congress to enact a
Copyright and Patent Statute if it saw fit. That provision did not itself have any independent legal force.

References in the debates of the Constitutional Convention to copyright are very sparse, few, and far be-

tween, so we don't really know much about what these
people thought they were doing, except that they associated copyright with, the phrase they used being, "for
the encouragement of learning." In fact, James Madison
and Charles Pinckney included in the Constitution, in
addition to the copyright and patent provisions, authorization to Congress to establish a National University.
On Pinckney's part, it was to establish seminaries for
the promotion of literature, the arts, and sciences.

For reasons that are not clear in the historical record, the provisions about the universities and the
seminaries were deleted somewhere as the clause worked
its way through the Committee on Detail, evolving to its
present form, which has been understood to authorize
congressional legislation in the area of patents and
copyright, although neither of those terms are used in
the Constitution itself. The constitutional phrase
speaks only of exclusive rights, leaving it to Congress
and then to the courts to figure out what exclusive
rights are or should be. The use of the word "secure"
as it pertains to authors in matters of their exclusive
right also was fraught with difficulty for the future.
It led to a great debate as to whether the purpose of
the provision was simply to protect or give security to
an existing common law or even natural property right
or whether it was to recognize and create a new right.
That question had agitated the courts of England in the
interim period, but we have no time to consider that
this morning. In any event, the very first Congress, the
Congress of 1790, did enact a copyright act along with
other new legislation. It was a very sparse, bare-boned
statute indeed. In fact, the very first thing that
should have been condemned under the new Copyright Act
was the act itself, because it was almost a verbatim
copy of the Statute of Anne.

If the Statute of Anne had been under copyright, its
copyright would have been infringed by the first American copyright statute. For "Lords, Spiritual and Tempo-
ral and Commons in this present Parliament Assembled,"
substitute "Senate and the House of Representatives of
the United States," and you have our first copyright
statute with but few other minor changes. There was even
the retention of the quasi-criminal provision of the

Statute of Anne, in that half of the recovery by a copyright owner for infringement of his copyright would redound to the United States, just as one-half of the recovery under the Statute of Anne had redounded to the Crown. The implementing statute of 1790 set an early format that has persisted in American copyright law until the new act of 1976. That is, it was a sparse, bareboned, skeletal affair which would tell a person reading it almost nothing about what it really meant. And that has been true of American copyright legislation from the beginning. Although some aspects are obviously provided for, such as the term of copyright and the very succinct description of the kinds of works that are eligible for copyright, the really difficult and profoundly philosophical questions have been left to be resolved by the courts. For example, no copyright statute has ever attempted to define or specify the quantum of originality that is required to hold copyright, nor to describe with anything more than the barest use of words, such as reprint, perform, or display, what is required to make out a case of copyright infringement. These have been left for the judges to deal with.

I don't want to imply that Congress was until 1976 wholly inert. Congress, by means of a series of amendments to the statute, had gradually broadened the category of works that were eligible for copyright. Originally only books, maps, and charts, again based on the Statute of Anne, could be copyrighted. In 1802, prints were included. In 1831, musical compositions were added and the term of copyright protection was increased to 28 years for the initial term, although the renewal term remained at 14 years. In 1856 dramatic compositions were added. A very important Congressional revision occurred in 1870 when Congress began the process of giving an extremely latitudinous interpretation to the meaning of the term "writing" as it appeared in the constitutional provision. That is, it included by statute for the first time three-dimensional objects, such as sculptures, molds, designs, and works of fine art. Until 1891 American copyright law had been extremely chauvinistic, giving no protection to foreigners. This was changed somewhat by an act passed that year, which for the first time permitted to foreign authors the benefits of Ameri-

can copyright protection, provided they complied with
all of the formalities of registration and deposit that
American authors had to comply with. It also provided,
and this was the kicker, that the compliance include a
manufacturing clause which required that any book in
English be manufactured in the United States to be eligible for copyright, creating an unsatisfactory state
of affairs, particularly for American authors who were
beginning to be read abroad and whose works were already
being pirated. This gave rise to more and more agitation
as well as a growing sense of need for the United States
to become integrated into the relatively new system of
international copyright protection. It was largely for
that purpose that a comprehensive revision was undertaken in 1909. However, that effort went pretty badly
off the track and produced a particularly horrendous
statute which has long been with us and which will in
fact continue to be with us until January 1, 1978.

Let me turn now for just a minute or two to the great
contribution of the courts. After the enactment of the
first copyright law in 1790, there was surprisingly little litigation about copyright for some 40 years or so;
in fact, there were only two cases prior to that of
Wheaton vs. *Peters* in 1834. In that year, a case of
enormous importance reached the Supreme Court of the
United States. A rather cozy affair, it involved a suit
for infringement by a former Reporter of Decisions of
the United States Supreme Court and his publisher
against the incumbent Reporter of Decisions, the incumbent having presumed to produce a condensed version of
the earlier Reporter's reports. A major question in the
case was whether there could be any copyright in decisions of the Supreme Court of the United States. However,
that turned out not to be the issue on which the case
was decided because the Reporter had added considerable
commentary and notes of his own which were susceptible
of holding copyright. The problem was that Henry Wheaton,
the former Reporter, had been a little careless in complying with certain rather complex formalities. I believe the formality in question was whether he had sent
the required number of copies of his reports to the
Secretary of State. Because he was doubtful of whether
he had, the question of law was whether that lapse would

invalidate his claim for copyright. However, the more important issue from the point of view of the longer historical perspective arose from the fact that Wheaton, sensing the vulnerability of the statutory claim because of his failure to comply with a single technicality, also brought a count for copyright infringement at common law. He claimed, as argued by Daniel Webster, among others, that even if his claim was invalid and his copyright was ineffective under the statute, he nevertheless retained a common law copyright.

Wheaton's counterclaim had required the Supreme Court, for the first time, to thrash out the vexed questions of the relative roles of the federal government and the state in the area of copyright, the relationship of the statute and the common law. This led, in the Court, to the opinions surveying much of the history that I've been relating so far, trying to decide again whether the purpose of the federal statute and the constitutional phrase which authorized it, was to secure (that was the word that was used) existing vested common law rights or whether it was to preempt the field and create a new statutory right which was exclusive of all others.

The question was quite important and acute at that time, because although we are familiar with the elementary proposition that common law rights and liabilities can be freely adjusted by legislation from time to time, it was not clear in the early nineteenth century whether, if there were such a thing as a common law property right, it could be abridged by any legislature, because that would be unconstitutional and contrary to natural right and justice. Wheaton's counsel made a very strenuous argument to the effect that there was such a thing as common law copyright, more or less in the keeping of the state (the state involved in this case was Pennsylvania), and that Wheaton could prevail on that theory. This was rejected by the Supreme Court in a four to two decision. There were only seven justices at the time and one was absent for illness. It was decided (and the main features of this decision have remained with us to the present time) that copyright, like patents, is primarily in the keeping and the jurisdiction of the federal government and such statutes as Congress may see fit to pass from time to time. The tipping point, that is, the point at which one loses one's common law or state rights to monopolize one's writings and other intellectual productions, is the point of publication. Once there is publication of a work, there must be protection under the federal law and the federal law only. This was extremely important, because if that had not been so decided, if it had been decided as Webster and others had argued for Wheaton that side by side with the federal statutory provision with its limited term was state law or common law, we could be confronted with a situation of perpetual copyright. Congress could say 28 years, or it could say the life of the author plus fifty years, but a state could provide for perpetual copyright and that would obviously make an enormous difference to the operation of libraries, among other things.

The next great development and contribution of the courts was what one might call the vulgarization or democratization (whichever you chose) of American copyright law. That is, there were in the origins of copyright considerable overtones of the belletristic. In other words, there were suggestions that in order to qualify for copyright, a certain degree of artistic or intellectual quality was required in addition to mere originality. That was made more plausible because a very considerable degree of ingenuity, sometimes described as a flash of genius, is required to hold the companion statutory monopoly, the patent. It might have been seriously thought that, when a claim of copyright was made, judges would undertake an examination of a novel or a magazine or a movie or whatever to decide whether it possessed the requisite quality of artistic or intellectual merit to hold copyright. In fact, as late as 1884, the Supreme Court of the United States intimated in a case involving a photographic portrait of Oscar Wilde, that in fact a certain degree of creativity and quality was required to qualify for copyright. Consider what matters would be like in our copyright universe had that idea persisted. If, for example, the question in a case involving the infringement of the copyright in *Playboy* hinged on whether *Playboy* promoted the progress of science or encouraged learning. Or whether, for a given potboiler novel, worth millions of dollars, the judges were called upon to decide whether the novel were good

enough, or artistic enough, or literary enough to qualify for copyright. It would be a very different sort of
copyright system and world we would be living in. That
has not been the case, and the reason it has not been
the case is most owing, ironically in a sense, to that
most patrician of our judges, Oliver Wendell Holmes, Jr.

It might seem odd that one of the most aristocratic
personalities in our history is probably more responsible than any other single person for this vulgarization
or democratization of copyright until one recalls
Holmes's constant impatience with Harold Lasky, who was
always urging him to spend his leisure time reading ed-
ifying, high quality books, as well as the fact that he
sought relief from the tedium of work of the Supreme
Court when he was in his eighties by frequenting the
burlesque houses of Washington. In any event, Holmes
believed it was too hopeless a task to inquire into
quality. He wrote in the *Bleistein* vs. *Donaldson* case
(and I will quote rather extensively from this opinion
because I think it had great influence on future developments): "It would be a dangerous undertaking for persons trained only to the law to constitute themselves
final judges of the worth of pictorial illustrations."
[This particular case involved circus posters, admittedly rather crude, unoriginal, and not particularly
artistic.] "...pictorial illustrations, outside of the
narrowest limits. At the one extreme some works of genius would be sure to miss appreciation. Their very nov-
elty would make them repulsive until the public had
learned the new language in which their authors spoke.
It may be more than doubted, for instance, whether the
etchings of Goya and the paintings of Manet would have
been sure of protection when seen for the first time.
At the other end, copyright would be denied to pictures
which appealed to a public less educated than the judge.
Yet if they command the interest of any public, they
have a commercial value and it would be bold to say
that they have not an aesthetic and educational value.
The taste of any public is not to be treated with con-
tempt. It is an ultimate fact for the moment, whatever
may be our hopes for change, that these pictures have
their worth and their success as sufficiently shown by

the desire to reproduce them without regard to the plaintiff's rights."

Vulgarization, democratization, or whatever you want to call that, the effect of this understanding of copyright accounts for the fact that copyright is the foundation of a multibillion dollar industry. Since that time, the courts have not inquired into quality. They have taken it as almost conclusive that if a defendent thought it worthwhile to plagiarize or pirate a work, it had sufficient commercial value. Commercial value is the ultimate fact for purposes of the validity of copyright, added to originality and compliance with the statutory categories.

That brings us to the background of the present Act, some details of which will be discussed by the speakers who follow me. I will just say a final concluding word to put it in historical perspective. It seems to me whatever else the 1976 Copyright Act does or does not do, whatever its merits or demerits turn out to be, it to a considerable extent marks the end of an era of judicial preeminence in the formulation of our copyright law. In contrast to its predecessors, going back to the first Copyright Act, the new law is lengthy, detailed in elaboration, and relatively specific. Considerable leeway for interpretation will still be left to the courts, such as working out the bounds of fair use under the general rubrics of Section 107, but considerably less will be left to the courts than previously.

The reason for this hardly lies in any newfound hostility to judicial lawmaking. On the contrary, never before has a nation apparently been so content to be governed by judges as has this nation in recent decades. The reason lies in the limits of the capabilities, the capacities, of lawmaking by adjudication. These limits were reached and surpassed by the burgeoning technologies with which you are all familiar. Judicial lawmaking is grounded in the processes of extrapolation from what is known and settled to the new issues encountered. Its method is that of analogy. As long as the technologies of copying and publication remained fairly stable, adjudication served us quite well. It was no great feat to analogize from piano rolls to phonograph records.

But the new technologies of mass reprography, cable TV, and computer programs have opened up gaps too large to be satisfactorily filled in by judicial technique and judicial reasoning, gaps whose closure can be accomplished only by legislative policy decisions arrived at by the Congress. If one had read the opinion in the recent Supreme Court's gasping effort, symptomatic of this final breakdown of lawmaking by adjudication, in *Williams and Wilkins* vs. *the United States*, which had to do with the mass reproduction of periodicals by the National Library of Medicine, one could sense the despair of the Justices who were unable to reach a decision other than the affirmation of the Court of Appeals by a divided vote of four to four. Their cry for help to the Congress was explicit. Now, after nearly twenty years of pushing, shoving, and hauling, Congress has addressed itself to the array of problems inherent in the old Copyright Act. It has made a mighty effort and has given us a rather different kind of copyright law than we have ever had previously. Whether the Congress has produced a mouse or a lion or a rational solution (whatever a rational solution might be) I will leave gladly to the speakers who follow me to enlighten us.

PROVISIONS FOR LIBRARY PHOTO-COPYING IN THE NEW COPYRIGHT ACT

THOMAS C. BRENNAN

My mission essentially is to set the stage for the subsequent presentations. I will be focusing on the evolution in the Congress of the library photocopying provisions of the new Act. My colleagues later will interpret, analyze, criticize, and dissect those provisions from different perspectives. When one is dealing with a statute as complex as the Copyright Revision Act of 1976, it is not adequate merely to read its provisions. One must become acquainted with the entire legislative history, including the committee reports. I often urge audiences to read those reports, but then I add the caveat that you probably will not find answers to the more interesting questions there. In fact, some of the commentary in the reports may even tend to point you in the wrong direction.

Professor Holland has provided a very interesting history of the development of the copyright system in England and the United States. It is clear that the primary purpose of the copyright clause in the Constitution was not to benefit authors but to advance the public welfare. The founding fathers and the Congress determined, however, that the public welfare would be served by the grant of a temporary monopoly to stimulate creative activity. In the recent legislation the

Chief Counsel, Subcommittee on Patents, Trademarks, and Copyrights, U.S. Senate.

Congress, in resolving a number of issues, had to bal-
ance the rights of the creators of copyrighted materials against the reasonable needs of the users of that
material. Probably the most fascinating of these balancing acts is the reprography question which is the
primary concern of this conference.

The initial issue that confronted first the principal parties and then the Congress was whether in fact
there should be a specific and detailed photocopying
section in the 1976 Copyright Act, or whether it should
be left to the application of the general provisions
of the fair use section. The early proposals of the
Copyright Office to include in the bill a library photocopying provision were criticized by all the interested parties. The library community opposed the proposals of the Copyright Office because they felt that
the 1909 statute and existing customs and practices,
including, if Bella Abzug pardons the expression, "a
gentleman's agreement," provided sufficient protection
for their activities. Authors and publishers likewise
opposed the proposals because they regarded them as an
erosion of their rights under the 1909 copyright act.
Consequently, at first it appeared that there would not
be a detailed photocopying provision in the statute.
This possible result led one commentator, Professor
Kaplan, to write: "The revision bill is reduced to ut-
tering on the subject only a staccato bleap of just the
words 'fair use.' It seems hardly a statesmanlike result to leave a sizeable fraction of the population
thus uncertainly subject to civil and even criminal liability for acts now as habitual to them as a shave in
the morning, especially as publishers are still far
from devising any simple methods by which the public
could calculate and make the payments that might legitimate these habits."

A few words now about fair use. There is no reference to fair use in the Copyright Act of 1909. As Professor Holland has previously explained, this defense
was developed by the courts. In essence, it provides
that certain uses of copyrighted materials for such
purposes as research, scholarship, teaching, comment,
and the like are not an infringement, in appropriate
circumstances, of the rights of the copyright holder.

Section 107 of the new Act undertakes to codify the
case law on fair use. The committee reports state that
the intention of the Congress is neither to expand nor
to contract the case law on fair use. Keep that in
mind. I'll come back to it later. The new statute provides four tests which should be applied in a particular case to ascertain whether that use is fair. Please
also bear in mind that certain library photocopying
practices will involve Section 107 as well as the special section on library photocopying.

The first of the four tests is the purpose of the
use. Is the use for a commercial activity or is it for
a nonprofit educational purpose? The second test refers
to the nature of the work. Obviously certain categories
of works require greater protection than others. The
third is concerned with the amount of the work being
copied in relation to the length of the entire work.
And the fourth considers the effect that the copying
may have on the commercial market for the work. During
much of the pendancy of the copyright bill in the Congress both the library community and the author and
publisher representatives were content to let the matter of library photocopying be determined by the application of those standards.

Into the situation now enters the publishing house
of Williams and Wilkins. As Professor Holland has indicated, Williams and Wilkins sued the United States
government, the National Library of Medicine, in the
Court of Claims, alleging that certain photocopying
activities of the library were an infringement of the
copyrights of the Williams and Wilkins Company. The
government had several grounds in its defense, one of
which was fair use. The trial commissioner found for
the plaintiff. The Court of Claims reversed the trial
judge in a four to three decision, holding that the
particular practices of the National Library of Medicine then before the court did not violate the copyrights of Williams and Wilkins and were a fair use.
The court indicated, however, that it was very uncom-
fortable in trying to resolve the issue based on the
Copyright Act of 1909 and indicated that it was engaged
in a holding operation until such time as the Congress
could adopt a legislative solution that took into ac-

count the various equities. One of the dissenting judges
on the Court of Claims described the court's decision
as the "Dred Scott case of copyright law." The Supreme
Court reviewed the case and, as Professor Holland indicated, one of the justices, Justice Blackmun, did not
participate in the court's decision. The Supreme Court,
by a vote of four to four, affirmed the holding of the
Court of Claims but that type of decision does not establish a precedent and thus, after several years of
litigation, the country knew as little about the federal
law as it did at the start of this exercise.

Consequently, during this period it became obvious
that the Congress would have to have a specific library
photocopying provision in the Copyright Revision Act.
We now have one. It began as one of the shorter provisions of the bill and it ends with nine subsections.
Several of these subsections of the statute's Section
108 are relatively noncontroversial. For example, the
Act permits a library or archive to reproduce an unpublished work in facsimile form for purposes of archi-
val reproduction; it permits the reproduction of a work
for replacement purposes when, after a reasonable effort
it has been determined that a copy cannot be obtained
at a fair price; it permits the reproduction of an entire work when the work is out of print and otherwise
unavailable; it exempts a library for photocopying activities on an unsupervised machine, provided the machine contains a notice such as "Photocopying may be
dangerous to the health of authors." Mr. Baumgarten will
enlighten you later as to what the Copyright Office is
contemplating with respect to the form of that particular notice.

The principal disagreement focused on the so-called
"single copy issue." The library associations, late in
the history of the bill, urged the Congress to incorporate into the Act a provision stating in substance that
it was not a violation of copyright for a library, directly or through an interlibrary loan, to furnish a
patron with a single copy of an article from a periodical or a reasonably short excerpt from an entire work.
When this amendment was proposed in the Congress it
received considerable support. However, author and publisher representatives were concerned that the wording

of the amendment contained the seeds of authorization
for wholesale library photocopying that could jeopard-
ize the viability of certain publishing activities as
well as deny authors a reward for their labors. This
issue was initially considered in the Senate subcommittee. The Senate subcommittee decided that the bill
should contain the single-copy authorization, but that
certain safeguards should be incorporated in the statute to prevent abuse. That was the origin of the now
famous prohibition of systematic reproduction and distribution. The Senate committee also felt that it was
not enough simply to have the statute talk about single
copies or prohibition of systematic reproduction, but
that there ought to be additional guidance given to the
library community and to others. This could not be done
in the statute, but it could be done to some extent in
the committee report.

Consequently, the Senate committee undertook, in
writing its report, to put some meat on the skeleton of
the statute. The subcommittee asked the parties to assist us in that exercise. We attempted to write into
the report an explanation of practices which were either
clearly prohibited or clearly permissible. Certain examples were brought to our attention which the committee
concluded did not qualify as the making of a single copy
and fell under the prohibition of systematic photocopying. Examples of these practices are found in the Senate committee report, and if you do not have a copy of
that document, I suggest that you attempt to obtain one
while it is still available. These prohibited practices
include the following illustrations which are taken from
the report: (1) If a library which has a collection in
a particular field, let's say biology, undertakes to
advise other libraries that they have the right to use
that collection and, as a consequence, other libraries
terminate subscriptions or refrain from what otherwise
might be a reasonable prospect of purchasing a subscription, this is regarded as systematic photocopying. (2)
In a library system with a number of branches, if the
branches get together and make agreements that one
branch will subscribe to certain periodicals and other
branches will subscribe to other periodicals, this is
another example of systematic photocopying.

We then turned to the interlibrary loan problem, and sought to obtain from the library associations an indication of what type of interlibrary loan practices they thought qualified as the making of a single copy. Unfortunately the library associations did not find it convenient to assist the Senate committee in this activity, and it was not possible to include in the Senate committee report a detailed discussion of interlibrary practices. However, I wish to emphasize that Section 108 does apply to interlibrary loans, and it was never the intention of the Senate to prevent or terminate interlibrary activities. I think possibly the reason the library associations were reluctant to assist the Senate committee and also others who were engaged in the same effort during that period was that hearings had not yet been held in the House of Representatives.

In any event, after the House hearings, an opportunity developed for a satisfactory and rational solution. The Congress had established a national commission to consider the impact of technology on copyright. This commission is focusing primarily on future problems, but it was also given certain jurisdiction in the area of library photocopying. With the approval of the Congress, the commission undertook to work with the parties in attempting to develop guidelines. The House committee amended the bill as passed by the Senate to add to the language of systematic reproduction a proviso that this prohibition did not include interlibrary loans which did not have the effect of replacing normal subscription activities. The commission worked with the parties and developed guidelines to interpret that proviso. These guidelines were essentially ratified by the Congress in the conference report on the new Act. Robert Frase will explain the nature of those guidelines.

The history of the bill clearly establishes that there are certain existing or potential library photocopying practices which the Congress believes exceed the scope of fair use or the exemptions of Section 108. The Congress has not sought to obstruct reasonable and prompt access to copyrighted materials but believes that in certain cases compensation to the copyright holder is justified. Consequently the Senate committee report states: "Concerning library photocopying practices not authorized by this legislation, the Committee recommends that workable clearance and licensing proce- dures be developed." It was for this reason that Sena- tor McClellan, who was the sponsor of the bill which became the new copyright act, wrote to the chairman of CONTU, that's the National Commission on New Technolog- ical Uses of Copyrighted Works, as follows: "I believe that it is important there be no disruptions in the use of copyrighted material by the patrons of libraries fol- lowing the coming into effect of S 22 because of the absence of appropriate clearance and licensing proce- dures for the types of photocopying practices not in- cluded within the exemptions of S 22. I therefore re- quest that the Commission, in conjunction with the formulation of guidelines, take appropriate initiative in coordinating the establishment of necessary clearance and licensing mechanisms." Senator McClellan's intent is that the commission lend its good offices to the de- velopment in the private sector of necessary permissions and clearance mechanisms. He has been assured by the chairman of the commission that this question is re- ceiving the active consideration of that body. It is to be hoped that procedures will be available prior to the effective date of the bill.

A separate but somewhat related question is the mak- ing of photocopies by libraries in commercial enter- prises. Both the Senate committee and the Copyright Of- fice concluded that a library in a commercial enterprise wishing to engage in copying beyond fair use should pur- chase the number of copies of the work that it requires or obtain the consent of the copyright owner to the mak- ing of the copies. One of several conditions which must be met by a library to qualify for the 108 exemption is that the reproduction be "without any purpose of direct or indirect commercial advantage." A number of corpora- tions and commercial libraries expressed concern at the positions taken by the Senate and the Copyright Office. The House of Representatives in no way altered the lan- guage of the Senate bill on this issue, but in its re- port, the committee somewhat strained to bring more li- braries in commercial enterprises within the scope of Section 108. The House committee indicated that isolated spontaneous making of single photocopies by such libraries is not deemed to be for a commercial purpose. A somewhat abbreviated statement of the House report language is incorporated in the Conference report. The Senate conferees were able to accept this language since it may well be construed merely as an application of the fair use criteria to the making of single photocopies by libraries and commercial enterprises. However, the history of the bill suggests that the criteria for this exemption should be strictly interpreted.

Finally, what is left of Williams and Wilkins after January 1, 1978? The holding in the Williams and Wilkins case, as you recall, was that the particular practices before the court in that case were a fair use. And you recall I said earlier that the committee reports on the new Copyright Act state that the Congress is codifying the existing state of the case law on fair use. It is neither contracting nor expanding the concept of fair use. It is my personal opinion that those general statements about fair use will be given very little weight by a court in resolving any litigation that may arise with respect to library photocopying. It is a well-established principle that when you have an earlier general statement followed by a later detailed statement, the latter is perhaps a more accurate reflection of the intent of the legislation. Therefore, I believe that a court in interpreting the Williams and Wilkins facts under the new legislation would look primarily to the history of the new Act, the committee reports and the debates in the Congress. It may well be that this history would require a different result than was reached in Williams and Wilkins.

DISCUSSION

Nancy Marshall (University of Wisconsin, Madison): With all the conference reports and now the committee reports, I would like to know, and I'm addressing my question to Tom Brennan, does the conference report, House Report 94-17-33, supersede the Senate report of November 1975?

Thomas Brennan: The chronology of this Act consists of
the Senate report, the House committee report, the
conference report, and any relevant debates. As to
conflicts, you must look to the latest expression of
the congressional will. There are some areas where
the conference report does undertake to resolve dis-
putes between the House report and the Senate report.
I think if I could possibly redraft the question you
are focusing on, the language in the Senate committee
report which discusses the interpretation of certain
aspects of Section 108 in relation to single copies
and systematic distribution, I would say that the
conference report does not supersede the language of
the Senate committee report.

Allen Willmert (Manchester College): My question is for
Professor Holland. Was there ever in the history of
copyright laws in England or in the United States
the issue or any litigation concerning the issue of
purity of text as the reason for copyright legislation?

Maurice J. Holland: Not to my knowledge, if I correctly
understand the term "purity of text." Does that mean
simply accuracy of . . .?

Allen Willmert: Yes, not changing the text with the same
title. The concern is, for example, today if someone
has devised an instrument for testing certain theses,
in psychology or something else, and somebody used
the instrument by altering its form, by altering questions in it, and so forth.

Maurice J. Holland: No, I guess on that understanding
I would repeat, no. As a matter of fact, the purer
the text, the greater the infringement. The more
scrupulously accurate the copying is, the more likely
that it would be held an infringement. The kinds of
concerns that you're getting at would, I think, be
covered by other branches of law that are relatively
undeveloped in this country, those dealing with mutilation or changes of works of art and literature,
perhaps even scientific works. In Europe the Law of
Moral Rights, something which we do not have in this
country, offers protection when, for example, someone

buys a high-grade picture painted by a fine artist, and displays it in some unsuitable manner, or even mutilates it or something of that kind. But no, I know of no copyright case that is concerned with purity of text.

Shirley Jenkins (Science Research Associates): My question is for Professor Holland. Concerning the manufacturing clause, if we publish a product in Canada, are we restricted in selling that product in the United States if we have not received a clearance in the contract for that product, you know by saying we want Canadian *and* U.S. rights?

Maurice J. Holland: I cannot answer that.

Herbert S. White: We have a table full of lawyers. Does somebody want to try that question?

Jon Baumgarten (General Counsel, Copyright Office, Library of Congress): I'll try a brief answer. As far as where you can distribute the work, I think that depends solely on your contract. If the contract gives you North American rights, then I don't think you have to worry about restricting yourselves to the border. I don't think that the question of the manufacturing clause and where you can sell it are necessarily one and the same.

Shirley Jenkins: All right, let me rephrase the question. We have maybe the same product, but we have a Canadian edition and a U.S. edition. If somebody wants to purchase the Canadian edition, simply for the very small difference in the language contained in that particular edition, are we restricted from selling that product in the United States?

Jon Baumgarten: Under the current law there are no restrictions if it was manufactured in Canada. Under the new law those restrictions will be removed if it was manufactured in Canada, assuming it's a work by an American author. If it's a work by a Canadian author, then even the problems under the current law are removed.

ROLE OF THE COPYRIGHT OFFICE IN THE NEW COPYRIGHT ACT

JON BAUMGARTEN

The role of the Copyright Office in the new Act is a matter about which there has been a considerable degree of confusion, both within and outside the legal community. I should point out the regulatory and related responsibilities of the Copyright Office under the Copyright Act of 1976. Although substantial and considerably broader than those existing under the current law, they are finite and are limited. We will not be serving as a government ombudsman of copyright. We will not replace legal counsel in questions of compliance with the law, nor will we otherwise exercise any wide-ranging authority. This is particularly true with respect to the enforcement of the rights of copyright owners, and the delineation of the limitations upon those rights, in the areas of library photocopying, educational copying, or any other. Generally, these are and will remain matters for private enforcement consideration and initiative among the parties affected.

The role that the Copyright Office will play under the new Act may be broken down into three categories: The first category, essentially in terms of time, is the regulatory implementation of the new Act; that is, the formulation and promulgation of regulations to fill out the statute where Congress has spoken in broad terms and specifically allocated to the Copyright Office the task

---

General Counsel, Copyright Office, Library of Congress.

of filling in specific details to the issuance of regulations. I must emphasize the words "specifically allocated" as a general matter and particularly in areas unrelated to registration responsibilities, about more of which I'll speak later. Where the statute itself does not expressly refer to regulations of the Copyright Office, we will not issue regulations.

I'd like to illustrate this by contrasting some textually related but administratively distinct provisions in Section 108, the well-known library photocopying section. At the same time, I hope to dispel some confusion that is apparently rather widespread, based on phone calls to the office. Paragraph a-3 of Section 108 requires as a condition of permitted reproduction that the reproduction include a "notice of copyright." No mention is made of Copyright Office regulations. Similarly paragraph f-1 of Section 108 provides that it shall not be taken to impose liabilities upon libraries for the unsupervised use of coin-operated machines if the equipment "displays a notice that the making of a copy may be subject to the copyright law." Again, no mention of Copyright Office regulations. Contrast this with paragraphs d-2 and e-2 of Section 108 that deal with the permitted photocopying of works or parts of works if, among other conditions, the library displays and includes on its order form a warning of copyright in accordance with requirements that the Register of Copyright shall prescribe by regulations. We will issue regulations under Section 108 d-2 and e-2 for the display and order form use of warnings, as directed in the statute. Our current thinking, however, is that we will not issue regulations for either the notice of copyright in paragraph a-1 or the legend to be put on photocopying machines under paragraph f-1. Nor, I might add, will we issue any regulations determining what is the fair price for the purpose of obtaining a replacement copy. Nor will we seek to extend or fill in or impose guidelines similar to the CONTU guidelines included in the conference report. These are matters for you to individually determine with your respective appropriate legal counsel and, in the area of guidelines at least, for further voluntary discussions among the parties. As Tom Brennan pointed out earlier, a request had been made to CONTU to participate in this.

The Copyright Office presumably also has some participation but not in the exercise of regulatory authority.
   The areas in which the Copyright Office will issue
regulations are, however, numerous and quite substantial. Beginning on January 1, 1978, the Copyright Law
of the United States will be fundamentally and basically changed. The old two-level system Professor Holland
referred to, with common law copyright for unpublished
works and statutory copyright for published works, will
be abolished in favor of a single federal system for
copyright for all works from the moment of creation.
Entirely new rules will govern the duration of copyright.
Authors will be invested with an entirely new termina-
tion right when they're dealing with publishers. Copyright liability will be imposed for the first time on
jukebox operations and cable T.V. systems. Public Broadcasting's liability will be clarified under compulsory
license existence. Similarly a complicated system will
be established for the use of copyrighted musical and
art works by noncommercial broadcasters. The system of
registering copyright claims and recording documents
affecting ownership of copyright and the Copyright Office will be continued, with several changes affecting
the significance of these acts and the classification
and application system under which the office will operate after January 1, 1978. All of these areas will
definitely involve the formulation of new Copyright Office regulations. In some, between now and January 1,
1978, every current regulation, practice, form, circu-
lar, procedure, or other piece of paper now used or
followed in the Copyright Office will have to be changed.
In addition, a number of entirely new concepts and responsibilities will have to be accommodated by the office, while at the very same time, in numerous individual cases, transitional applications of former procedures, former regulations, and former forms will still
be required.
   I'd like to turn for a moment to the procedures the
office will follow in developing these regulations. They
generally take one of two forms, each involving the
fullest possible public participation. Under the first
form we will issue in the *Federal Register* an actual
proposed regulation in the form of a document called

"A Notice of Proposed Rule Making" and we will ask for
public comment. In some of these cases we will ask for
public comment through written comment letters, in which
case we will generally give a deadline for the initial
comments and a deadline for the reply comments. In other
cases the comments will be solicited through oral hearings at the Copyright Office. After considering the comments, we will then issue in the *Federal Register* a final regulation, which will be accompanied by a full description of all the comments we have received, whether
we agree with them or not.

The second form of rule making is slightly different.
The first step will be to issue in the *Federal Register*
not a proposed regulation, but a statement of issues or
questions (either broad or detailed) on which we would
like public comment. This document will generally be
deemed or called "An Advance Notice of Proposed Rule
Making." Again we will ask the public to respond to the
advance notice and to the questions stated, either
through written comments or hearing as the advance notice directs. After considering the comments, we will
go to the stage of formulating a proposed regulation,
publishing that and again asking for comments on the
proposed regulation. Whether we select the first approach or the second approach depends on a variety of
factors. Perhaps the most significant of these is how
much outside input we feel we need before we can consider alternatives and come up with proposed regulations.
The second form is one we've used in an area that may be
of considerable significance to this audience. On March
30, 1977, we published in the *Federal Register* an advance notice of proposed rule making to solicit public
comments on the regulation relating to use and display
of copyright warning referred to earlier. This will be
the form of warning to be used by libraries on their
order forms, and at the place their orders are accepted.
For those of you who haven't seen it, following are some
brief excerpts. "This advance notice of proposed rule
making is issued to advise the public that the Copyright
Office of the Library of Congress is considering adoption of a new regulation pertaining to the use and display by libraries and archives of certain warning of
copyright in connection with photoduplication and re-

lated activities. The notice is intended to elicit public comment, views, and information which will assist
the Copyright Office in considering alternatives and
formulating a tentative regulation, to be later issued
as a proposed rule for additional comments. . . . All
comments relative to the content, use, and manner of
display of these warnings will be considered by the
Copyright Office in proposing a regulation. In addition,
information and examples are specifically requested with
respect to (a) the kinds of order forms currently used
by libraries and archives in relation to their photoduplication and related activities; and (b) the kinds of
copyright legends, warning, and the like currently in
use on order forms in photocopying machines and displayed in connection with photocopying and similar activities."

If you wish to comment and give us information in
this area, the initial deadline for comments to be received in the Copyright Office is May 6, 1977, and should
be addressed to me. After that, there will be a period
of approximately three weeks until May 23, 1977, when we
will have an opportunity to reply to the comments filed
by other parties. How do you find out about these proposed regulations without subscribing to the *Federal
Register*? If you wish, you can be placed on the Copyright
Office mailing list by writing to the office. Generally,
when the notice comes out in the *Federal Register* we try
to photo-offset and mail it to those on our mailing list
within one or two days after the notice appears.

The next or second category of the Copyright Office
role under the new Act concerns the formal administration of the statute which begins on January 1, 1978. In
this area, we're dealing with the familiar Copyright Office functions of registering claims to copyright and
recording assignments, exclusive licenses, and similar
documents related to copyright ownership and transfer.
Obviously, these actions will have to be in conformance
with the regulations formulated under our first described
role of regulatory administration. I do not plan to go
into this in any detail, other than to point out that
application forms and the classification system related
to registration after January 1, 1978, are likely to be
substantially changed. I'm beginning to learn what a

difficult job it is to devise a form which will be
understandable and usable. I hope we do a little bit
better than the IRS. I'd also note that the office will
not grant and has *never* granted copyrights. Under the
new statute, copyright will attach automatically upon
the creation of the work, that is, when it is first
fixed in a tangible and visually perceivable form. That
is how copyright will be acquired. The Copyright Office
will register the claims to the copyright which are
automatically attached to the work but will not grant
the copyright itself. This is a very basic and fundamental change in the new law which is not widely recognized.

Technically, after January 1, 1978, it will be entirely inappropriate to speak about copyrighting a work
or securing a copyright in a work. When the work is
created, that fixed copyright exists and it exists in
essence whether you want it or not. The question under
the new law will not be how to acquire a copyright but
how to avoid losing it. Under the substantially amelio-
rated provisions pertaining to copyright notice, it
will not be an easy thing to lose under the new statute.
In addition to registering claims to copyright and recorded documents of ownership, formal administration of
the statute will encompass several entirely new responsibilities. Believe it or not, the Copyright Office will
be engaged in licensing every jukebox in the United
States to perform copyrighted music. We will also be receiving statutory royalties from both jukebox operators
and cable television operators. The funds will be proc-
essed and accounted for in the Copyright Office, deposited with the Treasury Department, and distributed by
the Copyright Royalty Tribunal. An entirely separate
agency of the Copyright Office is due to be named by
the President. In addition, we will have the job of collecting obituary data and establishing records of the
identity and dates of deaths of authors for use in determining the duration of copyright. Under the provisions of the new law, in most cases, duration for works
created after January 1, 1978, will be measured on a
system based on the life of the author, fifty years after the author's death rather than from the date of publication.

The final category of Copyright Office responsibility under the new statute is, for lack of a better word,
a reportorial function. Mr. Brennan and his counterparts
in the House of Representatives were concerned that the
Copyright Office staff might not have enough to do. They
decided that in various as yet unresolved or in some yet
to emerge areas the Copyright Office should conduct
studies and report to Congress. One of the most significant ones I will mention, because it is perhaps the most
pressing, is whether there should be a performance right
for sound recordings. That is, essentially, whether
broadcasters and jukebox operators should pay record
companies and performing artists when their music is
broadcast or played on the jukeboxes. They currently pay
the owner of copyright in the music, the publisher, and
the composer. The question is now whether they should
compensate the performing artist and the record producer
for their creative contributions, a question that has
had a very long and controversial history in this country. The deadline for our report is January 3, 1978, two
days after we have to finish everything else. We intend
to go at it with full vigor.

There have been rumors in the trade papers that the
Copyright Office has already made up its mind in this
area because the Register of Copyright has testified in
favor of a performance right. However, we are committed
to a full, impartial, objective study of this issue. We
will be announcing hearings to be held in the near future. The hearings may appear on the West Coast, in New
York, and possibly in Nashville. Similarly, the members
of the Senate have requested the Copyright Office to
study and report to Congress by 1981 on what Professor
Holland referred to before as the anticipated phaseout
of the domestic manufacturing requirements of the new
Act. Phaseout is a word commonly but inappropriately
used, since the way the statute is now structured the
requirement will immediately and suddenly disappear in
July 1982. There will be no phaseout period. Members of
the Senate were concerned that the economic ramifications of this elimination were not entirely known and,
although it is in the statute, Senators McClellan and
Scott have asked us to look into the matter further and
issue a report to Congress sometime in 1981 about what

the anticipated economic effects will be. And under the
new law, the sale of American authors' books that are
manufactured in Canada will be permitted. However, that
was part of a deal worked out some years ago between
representatives of the Canadian and American publishing
industries. One of the quid pro quos was to have been
that Canada adhere to the Florence agreement for the
importation of books and remove its tariff barriers. The
Canadian government has not yet done so. Some members of
the Canadian publishing industry are beginning to take a
second look and are beginning to think that perhaps they
might have more to gain by the maintenance of tariff
barriers than they would by doing manufacturing for American publishers. Some of them are saying that they were
never party to the original agreement, which has conno-
tations for those of you familiar with the old gentle-
men's agreement that Tom Brennan mentioned. However,
we're still optimistic. Recently the Canadians issued
an entirely new report, paving the way for revision of
their copyright law. Therefore there still may be further developments in this area.

Perhaps of the greatest significance to this audience
in terms of our reportorial function is Section 108 i.
This section of the new Act requires that in January
1983 and at regular five-year intervals thereafter, the
Copyright Office, after consulting with representatives
of authors, publishers, libraries, and library users,
report to Congress on the extent to which the library
photocopying section of the new law has achieved the
workable balancing of the right of creators of copyrighted materials and the needs of users, and make recommendations as to further legislation if warranted.
Although this report is not due until January 1983, we
are aware that we can't sit back and wait. Some monitoring process has to be started, and we are considering ways of doing this at this time. The one step we've
already taken has been correspondence with the National
Center for Educational Statistics of HEW, discussing
with that agency the inclusion in its regular NCES library surveys certain specified questions related to
the photocopying activities of libraries. Libraries may
therefore see some new questions in the questionnaires
they'll be getting in the future.

A related matter of interest, I believe, although
not strictly a Copyright Office reportorial function,
relates to the very important issue of off-the-air recording of copyrighted materials for use in educational
institutions. The Copyright Act of 1976 has a limited
number of provisions dealing with off-the-air recording. Under Section 108 f of the new copyright statute
certain libraries are permitted to make a limited number of off-the-air recordings of audiovisual news programs. However, permission is limited to audiovisual
news programs, a concept about which there is some significant disagreement as to meaning. Similarly, under
Section 118 of the new act it was planned that educational institutions be permitted to engage in off-the-
air recording of certain works without the permission
of the copyright owner. However, such recording also is
extremely limited and extends only to music and to pictorial, graphic, and sculpture work included in the public broadcasting program being taped. Technically, a
library will still require permission of PBS or whoever
else might own the rights and the program as a whole.
Under the new statute virtually every television program
will be copyrighted from the moment it is recorded,
either before or simultaneously with the telecast. The
effect of Section 118 in essence is to say that if a library or educational institution gets the right from
Public Broadcasting after recording the program, it
won't have to worry about whether Public Broadcasting
has the rights to the music or to pictorial, graphic,
or sculptural work to grant. The statute gives libraries
and schools those rights. However, the statute in relation to Public Broadcasting gives libraries or schools
absolutely no rights whatsoever with respect to nondramatic literary works such as novels, poetry, or text-
books, or with respect to dramatic works such as plays.
Obviously, Sections 108 and 118 deal with very small
pieces of the off-the-air recording pie. It's no secret
that the off-the-air recording equipment now available
in educational institutions, media centers, and libraries is substantial and that a rather significant amount
of off-the-air recording is going on. There was an attempt during the later stages of the revision program
to try to resolve this problem, as is so well stated

in the report of the House Committee: "The problem of off-the-air taping for non-profit classroom use of copyrighted audiovisual works incorporated in radio and television broadcasts has proved to be difficult to resolve. The committee believes that the fair use doctrine has some limited application in this area. But it appears that the development of detailed guidelines will require a more thorough exploration than has so far been possible of the needs and problems of different interests affected and of the various legal problems presented. Nothing in Section 107 or elsewhere in the bill is intended to change or prejudge the law on this point. On the other hand, the Committee is most sensitive to the importance of the problem, and urges the representatives of the various interests, if possible under the leadership of the Register of Copyright to continue their decisions actively and in a constructive spirit. If it would be helpful to a solution, the committee is receptive to undertaking further consideration of the problem in the future economies."

That last phrase brings to mind the first draft of the House report which said something more definitive than "the future economies." The Copyright Office and the Register of Copyright have taken this paragraph of the House report most seriously. If I don't get any questions on off-the-air recording after this paper, it will be the first paper I've given dealing with any subject since January of 1976 in which the issue of off-the-air recording has not been raised. It's one issue we're constantly getting questions on, and as I say, we're aware of its significance. In July a conference will be held by invitation under the joint auspices of the Copyright Office and the Ford Foundation, directed not to solving this problem, which is somewhat too much to expect at this point, but to finding out what the real issues are. The Copyright Office will be writing to representatives of the educational community, the library community, broadcasters, the guilds, the labor unions, the publishers, and the authors in an effort to learn what the issues and the respective positions of the parties are.

DISCUSSION

Bill Heuser (Ball State University): In a section of the
Copyright Law it states that if you cannot acquire a
copy at a reasonable cost, that there are some provisions for copying with regard to off-air broadcasting.
We have tried to obtain a copy by any medium, either
television, videotape or motion picture, and they said
"yes" the material was available. Thus nobody engaged
in copying it. When we tried to acquire the material
the broadcaster said, "No it isn't going to be available, now or in the future." Where do we stand with
regard to protection of availability of material for
use?

Jon Baumgarten: I think that the portion of the act that
talks about availability of a copy at a fair price is
under paragraphs d and e of the library photocopying
provisions, which do not apply to audiovisual material
if I recall correctly. I think if a test case arose as
to whether off-the-air recording of a particular program was a copyright infringement or not, the court
might, as it's purported to do, and I underscore the
word *purported* in Williams and Wilkins, take into account the alternative forms of availability of the
material. However, you must recognize that the broadcasters who have maintained a very hard line in the
past claim that the material *is* available and that
they *are* marketing it. There may be some time gaps,
but that is one of their major concerns. If they were
not making it available, they'd claim at least that
they wouldn't really be worried about people taping
it off the air. I think that the degree to which it is
actually available in alternative forms is one of the
issues we hope will surface in July.

Roger Billings (Chase College of Law): I want to focus on
Section 110 which on the face of it doesn't seem to
speak to off-the-air recording, but I think does by
implication. Do you think so too?

Jon Baumgarten: It does speak to off-the-air recording,
but only in a very limited sense. That is, Section 110
is the . . . no, I'm sorry 110 itself doesn't speak

about off-the-air recording. It speaks about performances. You'd have to go to 112, the section which
gives you the right to tape something you already
have the right to perform, to get into any real deal-
ings with off-air recording. I think perhaps that's
the section you're talking of. Section 112 of the new
act, for those of you who are not familiar with it,
is a section derived from European jurisprudence.
It's called ephemeral recording. Some of the recordings that can be made under Section 112 can be kept
for seven years, which is not too ephemeral. The provisions of Section 112 are not, in my opinion, the
answer to the off-the-air recording problem. In the
first place they apply to making a recording of a
broadcast you've already acquired the right to perform, either under voluntary negotiations or under
the instructional broadcasting provisions. I don't
think they apply literally or on purpose to a media
center in a school recording a performance of "Roots"
off-the-air. Does that answer your question? If it
helps, I think it's the most we can expect.

Marina Griner (Fort Benjamin Harrison, Indiana): My
question refers to the American Society of Composers,
Artists, and Performers. How does this relate now
with the broadcasting problem in the copyright law?
Are they still making agreements for the release of
their works?

Jon Baumgarten: Oh, yes. The question was how the new
act affects American Society of Composers, Authors
and Publishers known as ASCAP, one of three performing rights societies. I shouldn't say three. There
could also be a fourth in this country. A little bit
of background: these societies own nonexclusive
rights with composers and publishers to authorize
performances of their repertoires. That will continue.
There's nothing to change that. In the public broadcasting area, in that area alone, there has been a
historical debate about whether ASCAP had the right
to license public broadcast performances or whether
those performances were exempt under the law. I'm not
going to get into that debate. There are people here
this afternoon who know more about it and could speak

very well to it. In that limited area the statute provides that if broadcasters can't get a voluntary license from ASCAP because now it definitely will be a royalty bearing performance, they may refer to the Copyright Royalty Tribunal for a compulsory license right. Other than that and some minor provisions related to (minor to this audience, not for ASCAP) loud speakers and fast food chains and religious broadcasts, the ASCAP/BMI system will essentially go on as it is.

CONTU'S ACTIVITIES AND SPHERES OF INTEREST

ROBERT W. FRASE

Both the staff of the National Commission on New Technological Uses of Copyrighted Works (CONTU) and the commissioners themselves are perfectly free to talk about what the commission has done and what it has agreed to do with respect to hearings and studies. Thus, as a member of the staff I cannot go beyond these ground rules and offer any personal views on issues. The commissioners, however, are free to state their personal views, if they so desire. First, I will provide a brief background on CONTU and then concentrate on its activities and concerns.

This commission is temporary and originally was given a three-year life span from the time of the signing of the copyright authorizing legislation, which took place December 31, 1974. That would have made the final report of the commission under the original statute due on December 31, 1977. However, the commission got off to a slow start because President Ford took about seven months to name the commissioners, so the commission recently went back to Congress and asked that those seven months be given back, thereby extending the final report date to July 31, 1978. The bill to accomplish this was approved by the House Judiciary Committee on April 6; it is expected to come up on the House floor in the

---

Assistant Executive Director, National Commission on New Technological Uses of Copyrighted Works.

very near future. So far it looks as if there will be
no opposition and the bill will be approved. The commission is an unusual combination. There are four part-
time commissioners selected from the general public;
four part-time commissioners selected from copyright
users, three of whom are librarians; four commissioners
selected from among copyright proprietors, three of whom
are publishers; and two ex-officio members, the Librarian of Congress with a vote and the Register of Copyrights without a vote.

The commission was given four specific areas to study
and on which to make recommendations back to the President and the Congress, both with respect to the possibilities of further changes in the copyright law and
with respect to copyright procedures. Three of those
issues relate to computers, and in view of the composition and interest of this audience I will mention them
only and not go into detail. These computer issues are
the copyrighting of computer programs, the copyrighting
of computer data bases, and the copyrighting of works
created with the assistance of computers. In the computer area the Congress said in the revision statute that
whatever the status now existing with respect to computers stays that way. The committee report states that it
stays that way until CONTU has had a chance to make recommendations and the Congress has had a chance to decide what to do about those recommendations. The fourth
area is concerned with reproduction, commonly called
photocopying, but it could be reproduction from microfilm into other microfilm, from microfilm to hard copy,
and so on. In that area the Congress did not stay with
the old law. It went ahead and made changes in the law,
but it also gave CONTU an opportunity to make further
recommendations.

The CONTU schedule as it appears now, that is, assuming that Congress will approve the extension of time
and that the final report will not be due until July 31,
1978, is to get out preliminary reports on these various subjects, invite comments, and possibly also receive
oral testimony on them before issuing the final report
and final recommendations. This will probably be done
first in the computer areas, in which the commission got
started earlier and did more work, setting aside the

photocopying issues until the Congress had finished its work on the revision bill. In the photocopying area there are a number of studies which the commission has either commissioned or has contributed to, or which exist independently of the commission but which will provide useful information to the commission and other parties as well and which will be taken into consideration for recommendations.

I'll just run over briefly what those studies are and as well mention that our publisher is the National Technical Information Service, the NTIS. All of the commission's hearings and its studies, as these are completed, will be available from that source. The first study is an analysis of 130,000 interlibrary loan transactions of the Minnesota state system, MINITEX, over the period of one year. This is an activity funded by CONTU by a grant of funds to the National Commission on Libraries and Information Science, which had earlier issued a contract to King Research of Bethesda, Maryland, to do a study of the photocopying activities of a sample of libraries and to design a royalty payment mechanism or mechanisms. This King Research study was the outgrowth of a recommendation of the Conference on Resolution of Copyright Issues, more commonly known as the "Upstairs Downstairs group," which represents both users and copyright proprietors. This group decided that they couldn't agree on substance but recommended that the study be done. The MINITEX tabulations, which will give a great deal of detail on the journals photocopied for interlibrary loan, the age of such material, whether the library borrowing has a subscription, and other things we don't know much about in detail now, should be available in the summer of 1977. For the full King Research study, the present timetable is July 15 for a preliminary draft of the report to NCLIS and a final draft of the report to that commission by August 15.

The second study is a survey of some 2600 scientific, technical, and scholarly journals with respect to their present practice and future ideas about providing or licensing authorized copies. This is contracted to the Indiana University Graduate Library School. The questionnaires went out a month or so ago, and as of the moment I think the school has something on the order of 700 back.

We expect a final report on that survey will be available about the end of June. We will make it available
promptly because it will be of great interest to others
who are working on this problem. The third study, by
Gene Palmour and Robert Vaughan, deals with comparative
costs of subscribing to periodicals and obtaining photocopies of articles through interlibrary loan. This is
an update of the 1968 study entitled "Library Cost Models: Owning vs. Borrowing Serial Publications" in which
Palmour was also involved. CONTU expects it sometime in
the summer of 1977.

The last of CONTU's projects is an analysis of the
copyright issues involved in computer and photocopying
from the point of the ultimate consumer and the general
public. This study is being conducted by the Public Interest Economic Center under the direction of Dr. Alan
Ferguson. Ferguson's report will then be placed before
two meetings of consumer and public interest group representatives convened by the Public Interest Satellite
Association, whose views will be solicited. The final
combined reports will be available to the commission by
July 1. The commission has been working since Fall 1976,
not as a committee of the whole but by setting up specialized committees of commission members. The Photocopying Committee, as does each of CONTU's committees,
consists of one public member, one member selected from
among copyright users, and one member selected from
copyright proprietors. The Photocopying Committee consists of Professor Melville B. Nimmer of the University
of California in Los Angeles and the vice-chairman of
the commission as the public member, Alice E. Wilcox,
Director of MINITEX, as the user member, and the author
John Hersey as the proprietor member. The committee is
now being expanded to include Robert Wedgeworth of ALA
and Dan Lacy of McGraw-Hill.

An important contribution that Tom Brennan referred
to came about outside the statutory responsibility of
CONTU, and was taken on as an extracurricular activity -
assisting the Congressional committees which were working with the interested parties in devising some guidelines for interpreting the provisions concerned with
interlibrary loan copying in Section 108 g-2 of the
bill. The commission offered its good offices to the

Congressional committees in April. The offer was accepted and CONTU started work on it. After some internal discussion, the commission came up with a first
draft of guidelines. This is an illustration of the
value, in this instance at least, of having commissioners from both proprietor and user groups. They quickly
arrived at a first draft which was then tried out on
library and publisher organizations. Several drafts
later the commission arrived at guidelines which satisfied the commission and the library, publisher, and
author groups. The guidelines were turned over to the
Congressional committees who accepted them and incorporated them as a reasonable interpretation of that part
of the statute in the conference report. The heart of
the matter was interpreting that provision which prohibits systematic photocopying, but permits "interlibrary arrangements that do not have, as their purpose
or effect, that the library or archive receiving such
copies or phono records for distribution does so in
such aggregate quantities as to substitute for a subscription to or purchase of such works." The question
is what are such "aggregate quantities." With respect
to interlibrary loans, the commission guidelines say
that the aggregate quantity which goes over the limit
is six photographic copies of articles from a single
periodical within a year, of articles in the last five
years of that periodical title. As to small portions
from nonperiodical materials there is no limitation on
the period. This limit does not apply if the library
borrowing a work owns a copy. The commission, however,
did not arrive at an agreement on guidelines with respect to copies from periodicals more than five years
old and did not deal with several other parts of Section 108 about which questions still exist. These
guidelines are, of course, available not only in the
Conference report, but in various other sources, including the very good special November 15, 1976, issue
of the ALA *Washington Newsletter* on the new copyright
law, which I understand has been widely distributed.
They may also be incorporated in materials relating to
a new standard interlibrary loan form being developed
by ALA.
    As for CONTU activities on photocopying, it has held

only three hearings devoted primarily to photocopying,
in October 1976, January 1977, and March 31-April 1,
1977. Those hearings, among other things, dealt with
library photocopying carried on by the British Libraries Lending Division at Boston Spa and such libraries
as Linda Hall in Kansas City, the National Library of
Medicine, and the National Agricultural Library. At the
March 31 hearing the Association of American Publishers
and associated groups outlined the plan to set up a
copyright clearance center for licensing and authorizing photocopying. Future hearings scheduled will probably also include photocopying. One is to be held May
5-6, 1977, and the other, July 11-12, 1977. A number
of library associations have formed an ad hoc Committee
on Copyright which is chaired by Frank McKenna of the
Special Libraries Association. CONTU has been corresponding with that group which has indicated that its
representatives would prefer not to come in to testify
and give us their advice, position, and point of view
until after they have seen the King Research studies
and some of the other studies the commission has under
way. It looks, therefore, that they may not come in and
testify until a fall meeting.

Out in the real world are some developments that are
significant to the commission. One is the Association
of American Publishers' proposed copyright clearance
center which you'll hear more about. The other is an
experimental program soon to get under way at the National Technical Information Service in which NTIS
would supply to its deposit account customers' authorized copies of periodical articles for a standard $6
fee per article. These copies would be supplied on the
basis of contracts which the NTIS would make with journal publishers and the various suppliers providing the
actual copies. NTIS would be sort of a middleman, receiving orders by teletype, forwarding the orders to
the supplier, and billing their deposit account customers. There is also a very ambitious plan for a National
Periodicals System which has been recommended by a special panel to the National Commission on Libraries and
Information Science. This will be published soon by the
Government Printing Office for the National Commission
(CONTU) and distributed widely for comment. An important

part of the plan, especially from the point of view of
copyright and the commission, is a central periodical
bank of some 45,000 periodicals and other serials, simi
lar to that of the British Lending Library Division at
Boston Spa, to be administered and funded after an experimental period by the Library of Congress. There are
also at present organizations in the business of supply
ing authorized copies, notably the Institute for Scientific Information in Philadelphia and University Microfilms.

A spate of foreign studies on photocopying also has
appeared, among which are a study by the Franki Committee in Australia which made a very liberal recommendation with respect to copying by libraries and education
al institutions, and an even more recent report of the
Whitford Committee in Great Britain which was presented
to Parliament in early March. The latter is a report
dealing with recommendations for a complete revision of
the British Copyright Laws, which are by no means confined to photocopying. The Whitford Committee took a
rather sweeping stand on photocopying, recommending tha
all photocopying be subject to copyright; but that ther
be no liability on anybody making photocopies until the
proprietors are organized to supply authorized copies
or licenses.

Yet another is the Keyes-Brunet Report in Canada
which deals also with a general revision of the copyright law. This proposes no special provisions on library photocopying, and again recommends that copyrigh
proprietors become organized and prepared to supply li
censes or to authorize photocopying. There is also a
Dutch law which is similar in some respects.

To supply data that will make it possible for the
Copyright Office to make its five-year report in 1983
on how library photocopying provisions of the Act have
worked out, CONTU has arranged with the National Cente
for Educational Statistics to include some questions o
library photocopying in its regular library surveys,
which the commission will pay for while it is in exist
ence. The Copyright Office will pay for this after the
commission is out of existence. To allay any fears, th
commission is not asking libraries to keep a detailed
record all year long. What is wanted is information on

the kinds of photocopying a library does in a typical
week during the year, and there will be plenty of advance notice before this information will be required.

DISCUSSION

Jim Self (Indiana University): The commission was unable
to decide what kind of guidelines to come up with for
periodicals over five years old. Is there any expectation that any agency or group will offer any kinds of
guidelines or advice on this topic?

Robert W. Frase: For this question I can give you a partial answer. Irwin Karp of the Authors League, who is
on this program, appeared before the commission at its
January meeting and had a list of questions as to what
the commission intended to do, and one of the questions
was whether the commission proposed to get into this
area of further guidelines for a periodical article
over five years old. The commission discussed the matter, and at its February meeting gave an answer to Mr.
Karp in a letter which is also included in the commission record, that they didn't know at this time. They
didn't say they would or they wouldn't - so the question is still open. It also raises a question. Suppose
the commission did get together with the parties and
arrived at something which was mutually acceptable. It
probably would have little more force of law or influence (and I defer to Jon Baumgarten on this) than if
the parties themselves had gotten together, because
the impact of the CONTU guidelines in the first instance came only because they were accepted by Congress
and put in the conference report.

Dale Middleton (Health Sciences Library, University of
Washington, Seattle): I have a question for both Mr.
Frase and Mr. Baumgarten. The Health Sciences Library
is also a Regional Medical Library. My question relates to the five-year review and the way in which we
might tool up to provide information for the five-year
review. I'm disturbed because I don't see the perti-

nence of the information I expect to be collected from this data-gathering effort. I don't see the pertinence in resolving or balancing the interests of creators and users. Can you speak to how you see it as pertinent and to what other things might be pertinent?

Robert W. Frase: I'm sure that there are other things that are also pertinent. All this will give you is statistics over a period of time. Take the higher education library survey as an example, starting this year and then three years later or maybe five years later, there will be statistics as to the volume of library photocopying of periodical articles and from books both for internal use and for inter-library loan. It will just show you what's happened to the growth. I'm sure there are other things that have to be taken into consideration, and I'm sure that the Copyright Office would be happy to receive suggestions from the library community as to what kind of data should be collected in these intervening years.

Jon Baumgarten: I think that Bob essentially answered the question. The five-year inquiry is not written out of whole cloth, but is designed to find out whether Section 108 works as it is now written. I was interested that in stating the question you seemed to emphasize the word creators, which is a little unusual coming from an audience of this nature. I was wondering if there was something in your question that was directed toward the authors that we really didn't catch.

Dale Middleton: Yes there is. Perhaps this is a biased view of my own. I don't identify particularly in the scientific journal area, I can't make the identification of the interests of authors with the interests of publishers.

Jon Baumgarten: I think perhaps Irwin Karp will speak to that. I think they [authors] have a common interest in the dissemination of information. There used to be, particularly in the days of Williams and Wilkins, all this talk that academics don't write for

profit, anyway. They would be just as happy to see
that everything they wrote was widely disseminated
through photocopying, that they couldn't care less
about the money. They tended to ignore the fact that
even nonprofit publishers have to recoup their in-
vestments in order to continue publishing. Indeed one
of the amicus curiae in Williams and Wilkins was there
on behalf of The American Chemical Society, which I
believe was the one who pointed that out. If you're
suggesting that the authors of such academic works are
more in the librarians' camp than they are in the publishers' camp, I wonder if that's really true if you
look at what nonprofit publishing is all about and how
it's done. Tom Brennan mentioned something earlier
which I'm always a little shaky about when I hear it,
but many of us say it. That is that the principal
beneficiary of copyright under the Constitution is the
public and not the author, but the Constitution does
tell you that you secure the public benefit through
rewarding authors. There's a tendency to equate public
interest with public access, but as Bob Frase pointed
out, the real public interest is in balancing between
public access and private ownership. I just don't see
the breakdown between publisher and author even in
your field that you might feel there is. You're presumably more the expert than I am.

Ronald Naylor (University of Houston): I have a practical
question which relates to the way in which libraries
do photocopying for their clientele. A researcher in a
branch library wishes to make a photocopy of an article
that he has learned about from a journal held in the
main library. He does not wish to come to the main library himself to make that photocopy which, as I understand Section 107, he will be permitted to do under the
terms of fair use. He will call or have his librarian
call the main library to make that copy for him and
send it to him by campus messenger. In what situation
does the library then find itself in relation to Section 108 g-2? Does this construe that it's intra-
institutional copying? Is it construed as interlibrary
loan? If it is intra-institutional, is it construed as
being in lieu of subscription by the branch library?
The questions could go on for a long time.

Robert Frase: According to Tom Brennan, who is more familiar with the Congressional intent, a branch will
probably work out to be the same library, so it is
not interlibrary loan. The second question concerns
something that nobody has interpreted, and that is
Section 108 g-1 which deals with systematic copying.
As I say, nobody offered any advice on that, though
this is also one of the questions which Irwin Karp
put to the commission. The commission didn't say yes
or no. The commissioners may get back to it.

Hardy Carroll (Western Michigan University): One of the
contentions of the National Library of Medicine in
the Williams and Wilkins case was that it was not in
the business of collecting money which would go to
private publishers. The federal government should
not be in that business. Now with what the NTIS and
maybe the Library of Congress is thinking about, is
there any indication that Congress is likely to accept this role of federal agencies in collecting
money which would go to private for-profit publishers?

Tom Brennan: If you like, in some of the other sections
in the Copyright Act there might be some precedent.
Other sections now involve the federal government in
the collection and distribution of royalties paid by
cable television systems and jukebox operators. So
there would not appear to be any unsurmountable
philosophical problem.

Hardy Carroll: Just one other point. The NTIS and Library
of Congress would supposedly be in competition with
the Institute of Scientific Information and University
Microfilm. Right?

Tom Brennan: That, of course, is another aspect of the
question. The NTIS question arose with regard to the
efforts to secure copyright in their own publications
on a limited basis. That was finally eliminated in
the conference committee, with some language in the
report that this problem ought to receive further
study in a future Congress.

THE NEW COPYRIGHT ACT: IMPACT ON TRENDS IN INFORMATION TRANSFER

LEE G. BURCHINAL

First, and very briefly, I will summarize copyright developments related to the dissemination of government-sponsored research. Second, and in a little more detail, I will suggest some trends, which, when taken with possible developments abetted by the recent copyright legislation, represent portents of the future. I will conclude with a few remarks about the implications of the forecasts for federal government policies and practices.

Impacts on dissemination of government-sponsored research. First, let us understand a few dimensions of government-sponsored research.

1. Such research is a major government activity. In 1976, your government spent $20.2 billion on R&D.
2. Of the $20.2 billion spent by federal agencies in 1976, over 60 percent ($12.2 billion) went for development activities. Copyright is irrelevant for most activities carried out under these expenditures. Activities are engineering-oriented. Results are encoded in hardware, to use Tom Allen's distinction with the verbally encoded results of research. Patents and patent policy are the big issues.
3. Approximately 40 percent of the federal R&D ex-

Director, Division of Science Information, National Science Foundation.

penditures in 1976 ($8.1 billion) went for sup-
port of basic and applied research. This is still
big money. Copyright is relevant here, because
the output of this activity is in the main verbally encoded and produced in such printed forms as
journal articles, technical reports, books, and
the like.

4. Research funds are concentrated in a few agencies.
Five agencies - HEW, DOD, NASA, ERDA, and NSF,
and in that order - account for about 80 percent
of the research funds expended by all federal
agencies.

Now let's look at how the recent revisions in copyright affect the dissemination of the results of federally conducted and sponsored research. A few brief remarks are sufficient to outline the present situation.

Federal publications remain in the public domain. Included are magazines and journals, abstracting/indexing
periodicals, books, reports, and other publications issued by federal agencies.

Two agencies attempted to secure authority to copyright their publications. The Department of Commerce
sought such authority for NTIS publications to help NTIS
in its effort to become economically self-sufficient.
NASA recommended that copyright in government be permitted in exceptional cases where such protection would be
essential to effective dissemination of results. Both
were unsuccessful, but NTIS did obtain a promise by Congress to hold further hearings on its request. This issue, therefore, is still alive.

Congress went about as far as it could go in seeking
copyright for U.S. works abroad under the "national
treatment" concept. That is, if other governments copyrighted their works, works of the U.S. government could
be afforded the same protection in those countries, provided the U.S. government asserts its claim to copyright
for uses outside the U.S. NTIS is now doing this. So is
the National Library of Medicine with respect to its
Index Medicus. This may be the start of a trend.

Copyright for privately owned publications in which
the results of federally sponsored research are reported
is continued, perhaps even strengthened. In Section 101

of the bill, "work of the U.S. Government" is narrowly
defined as "a work prepared by any office or employee
of the U.S. Government as part of that person's official
duties." Otherwise, barring any other limitation included in the award agreement, results from federally sponsored research published privately can continue to be
copyrighted.

This is a significant development. Over two-thirds
of the results of federally sponsored research - the
value derived from our $8.1 billion in taxpayers' dol-
lars - are communicated by means of privately owned
journals. This means that journal publishers can continue to enjoy copyright protection for works based on
government-sponsored research.

Beyond copyright legislation, however, policies and
practices of agencies influence dissemination activities. For example, all agencies reserve the right for
royalty-free license for reproduction of material resulting from federally supported publications. In addition, DOD arranges for dissemination through NTIS of
reprints of published articles based on research supported by that agency.

Finally, federal libraries and employees will be affected in the same way as all other libraries by eventual developments related to photocopying.

Copyright developments and the broader milieu. Copyright is only one change among many that are simultaneously shaping the evolution of information transfer
activities in the United States. Let's look at a few
of the significant trends. Selection of a set of trends
probably tells as much or more about the analyst as
about the phenomena being analyzed. Recognizing this
hazard, I offer the following five trends as particularly relevant to our discussion:

1. Continued steady increase in the amount and variety of material imposed on the U.S. information
   transfer enterprise. Output in science and technology continues to rise. Worldwide growth rates
   are approximately twice that of the United States.
   A rule of thumb is that the worldwide volume of
   scientific and technical publications continues
   to double every eight to ten years. Increases are

occurring in other fields as well. Moreover, the
forms of reporting and distribution are becoming
more varied, including print, microforms, electronic, and audio media.

2. Search for increased cost-effectiveness in managing this ever-increasing volume and diversity of
material. While costs continue to rise, communications technology offers lower unit costs and possibilities of increased effectiveness. Consequently, our enterprise is turning to automation, following the lead of other industries. Many labor-
intensive operations are being modified, if not
replaced, by capital-intensive methods. In this
sense, our miniscule portion - the library and
related information services component of the
larger U.S. information processing industry - is
following precedents established in commercial
information industries, such as banking and insurance, reservation services, and corporate research
management and communication. Library automation,
on-line bibliographic searching, and computer-
directed typesetting for publications represent
first-generation applications. Further improvements are promised by distributive networking
arrangements.

But other changes are over the horizon.

3. Structuring of the market by organizational buying
behavior. As the information transfer enterprise
becomes more costly, capital-intensive organizations, not individuals, are becoming the chief buyers. Capital outlay decisions generally require
authorization at higher levels in the organization.
Greater and more convincing documentation about
cost-effectiveness is demanded as well. Criteria
for cost-effectiveness are taking a turn as well,
away from benefits to the library or information
center to demonstrated value in terms of contri-
buting to the goals of the organization.

4. Emergence of information managers in large organizations. As choices become more complex and involve
larger sums, organizations are beginning to develop
information or communication management roles.

5. Expansion of fee-based services. With increased
   costs, greater automation, and associated capital-
   intensive operations, new sources of revenue will
   be necessary to sustain the more costly but probably more cost-effective services available to
   users. Increased public funding to meet these
   costs is not likely. More likely, users will be
   required to pay at least part of the costs of more
   sophisticated services in the future. Trends are
   already well established. Federal agencies are
   seeking at least partial cost recovery. Some, like
   NTIS, are committed to full cost recovery. Libraries are charging for use of on-line services.
   Profit-seeking "information on-demand companies"
   have successfully entered the field.

With reference to point 4, the chief contenders for
these roles likely will be directors of data processing
centers, since higher level management mistakenly
equates improvements in communication with more sophisticated computer-based systems. Directors of library and
information services, of course, are in a favorable position to compete for these roles as well.

With their purchasing power, these individuals will
probably become important new forces in shaping the mix
of products and services offered. For example, information managers may wish to purchase hard copy or COM-
generated fiche of articles meeting a certain profile
rather than to subscribe to so many copies of journals
and to provide copies to users on demand through internal corporate facsimile networks. Others may want output
in electronic form. Corporate information managers will
find ways of articulating and aggregating demand for new
or varied products that are lacking today.

As for point 5, development of new forms of demand
will also present publishers with opportunities to bundle services and pricing. Journals and microfiche can
be priced as a bundle. Purchase of journals with specified rights for reproduction represents another bundling
possibility. Bundling possibilities should serve to encourage greater flexibility in products and pricing.
This should have the dual effects of benefiting subscribers and ultimate users by giving them a greater

variety of choices in the media and format used to convey information as well as opening new revenue sources
for publishers.

Copyright revision in this milieu. In this milieu,
the most relevant provisions of the new copyright law
are the restrictions on systematic copying. Operation-
ally, these provisions will be eventually translated
into some kind of remuneration paid to copyright owners
for systematic copying. Effects of such a development
will probably include:

1. Further increases in costs for information. Organizations or individual users will pay to obtain materials they had obtained free or at lower
   costs.
2. Increased trend toward use of fees for services.
   Many organizations no doubt will pass along costs
   on to users. Breaking the "fee" barrier may have
   a snowballing effect, leading to charges for at
   least some other services.
3. Further increases in cost-consciousness. As costs
   are imposed for copying, librarians and users
   will become more sensitive to the economics of
   information access. Greater discrimination in what
   one thinks one needs likely will result.
4. Further impetus to find more cost-effective methods for accessing and delivering information. As
   costs increase and librarians and users become
   more discriminating, there will be greater emphasis on implementing cost-effective improvements in
   information delivery. The search for improvements
   will take many forms. One result probably will be
   increased document-on-demand publication. This
   will occur as libraries specify more clearly their
   core document collections and rely on other sources
   to satisfy requests for less frequently demanded
   materials, much of which may be stimulated by on-
   line bibliographic services. Also, some libraries
   may, for cost-effective purposes, shift from paper
   holdings, even for core materials, to microform
   holdings, from which distribution copies can be
   produced in paper or on fiche, and perhaps at different prices. As space and energy costs mount,

micrographic storage with reproduction on film or
paper on demand will become more attractive. In
time, with advances in microform facsimile and
electronic transmission, full document delivery
directly to the place of work will become common.

5. Greater competition among intermediaries that
stand between suppliers and ultimate users. Libraries and information centers have had this
field pretty much to themselves. In the future,
as information becomes accepted as a commodity
and is priced in the market place, buyers will
tend to shop around more and look for the most
cost-effective offerings. Just as food services,
security, and other services, so at least some
library, reference, referral, searching, and other
information retrieval services may be purchased
by organizations from specialized outside sources.

These changes are likely to be abetted by some form
of copying fee. Automated means for on-demand delivery
may be one way of curtailing costs and automatically providing for reproduction fees while increasing effectiveness from the perspective of users.

Record keeping, a by-product of on-demand services,
will also facilitate more cost-effective management of
library and information services.

Harbingers of these trends will likely appear first
in libraries and information centers serving industrial
users.

Implications for government action. Here I offer further conjecture intended to sensitize us to some developments which could have impacts across the entire information transfer enterprise. For starters, here are a few
implications for consideration by government decision-
makers:

1. Reconsideration of the roles of federal agencies
in information dissemination. Current pressure to
achieve cost recovery could well become translated
into justification for any operational activity in
light of the growing commercial value of information and the corresponding increasing role of the
private sector in dissemination of information
based on federally sponsored research.

2. Rethinking of the organization of federal dissemination efforts. Distributive networking, based on computer and micrographics technologies offers alternatives to centralized dissemination methods, represented by GAO and NTIS as well as the National Periodical Center. Available technology can permit microfiche facsimile reproduction. Agencies with large fiche files, such as NTIS, ERDA, NASA, and ERIC, could be linked for remote display or reproduction of fiche held by these or other centers. Document-on-demand reproduction, of course, can be extended to any set of materials, and be combined with on-line bibliographic searching.

3. Revision in federal research grant policy related to dissemination of results. Federal research grants provide two kinds of support: (a) up-front money to facilitate the dissemination of research results; and (b) transfer of finances to help libraries meet their burdens. The former (a) is achieved by reimbursement for costs of publishing articles in journals owned by not-for-profit organizations. Referred to as page charges, this amount comes to about $13 million a year. Support for improving access to available information (b) is more complicated. Research awards carry an indirect cost rate, part of which is earmarked for support of libraries at the institutions conducting the research. Federal funds involved are estimated in excess of $150 million annually.

In time, as the information transfer enterprise becomes more automated and connects with individual users at their places of work, whether office or laboratory, federal policies for support of dissemination may have to be revised. Instead of supporting publication at the front end, federal funds could be channeled through users - the researchers - or their surrogates, libraries. Under this arrangement, costs for communication, including on-line searching and direct document delivery could join costs for other computer services. Preparation of materials for publication could become direct-cost items in the research budget. Researchers could select which service they want or could aggregate funds through their

library and allow the library to use its combined purchasing power to obtain the best possible deal in the
market place.

Such changes are a long way off but are not inconceivable, especially as on-line searching moves beyond
bibliographic access and is extended to include remote
document and numerical data delivery.

Conclusion. Our murky crystal ball allows few conclusive forecasts. Certainly, as copying fees become
institutionalized, behavior will change. Publishers may
choose to alter the format and media of publication to
meet new market conditions and user behavior. Buyers
and users will encounter new and different cost and opportunity situations. Motivations and rewards for various sets of authors, publishers, buyers, and users will
continue to differ.

Accommodations will be sought and achieved among
these divergent groups. These accommodations will include adaptation to behavior changes abetted by new
legal requirements that will emerge from interpretation of the new copyright law.

In retrospect, a decade hence, it may turn out that
the copyright issues, so intense now, were only a symp-
tom of adjustment to far more fundamental changes in
the methods used to sustain economically viable and
cost-effective methods for transferring information.

THE AUTHOR'S VIEW OF THE NEW COPYRIGHT ACT

Having participated in my share of symposiums on copyright and other problems that afflict authors, I realize that the selection of titles is a thankless task. "The Copyright Dilemma" is no exception. The *American Heritage Dictionary* gives as its first definition of dilemma "a situation that requires one to choose between two equally balanced alternatives." That definition does not work for copyright. The Copyright Acts of 1909 and 1976 present a myriad of situations, and few if any of them permit one to choose between two equally balanced alternatives. The second definition is perhaps more accurate, but it is too pessimistic: "a predicament that seemingly defines a satisfactory solution." In any event, the history of the 1909 Copyright Act, no matter what you may have been told about it, demonstrates that many difficult predicaments yielded to solutions, and that many of the solutions worked, which is a pragmatic definition of "satisfactory." The last primary definition of dilemma, according to *American Heritage,* is an argument in which an antagonist is presented with "a choice of two or more alternatives, each being conclusive and fatal." That does echo some of the rhetoric in the congressional hearings on the revision bill. On several issues, if both sides were to be believed, the choices all

---

General Counsel, Authors League of America.

would be fatal. This definition is not much of a spring-
board for a symposium, for if every path leads to disaster, why spend two days talking about it.

In reality, there is no such thing as a copyright dilemma. The copyright revision bill and the copyright act
that emerged from it, as did the 1909 act, present a
number of separate distinct issues and problems so distinct that the antagonists who faced each other on one
issue had little or no interest in other issues. For example, those who fought over cable television and who
managed to hold up the bill for at least five or six
years had little concern with anything else in the entire statute. The large number of organizations which
testified in the hearings is explained in part by the
fact that many offered views on the one or two sections
which affected their constituents.

The reason the Authors League made more appearances
before the subcommittees than any other organization is
due simply to the circumstance that many more provisions
of the copyright law affect authors of dramatic and literary works than any other group of users or creators.
Our organization is the national society of professional
writers. Our members write books, plays, poetry, journal
articles, and other works for both publication and performance. A goodly number of them also practice other
professions. They include teachers, editors, business
executives, lawyers, and even librarians, so that we are
not afflicted by tunnel vision on the problems of the
copyright law.

What then are the implications of the new act for
the community of writers and dramatists? Let's consider
first the implications of the law in terms of the constitutional purpose of copyright, a bit of which was
presented to you by the first speaker. Actually, we are
not in the dark and do not have to depend on legal his-
torians to explain the purpose of the law. We can look
to the Supreme Court, which very explicitly told us
that the philosophy underlying the copyright clause of
the Constitution is "the conviction that the encouragement of individual efforts by personal gain is the best
way to advance public welfare through the talents of
authors."

The point, as the court said, is that the instrument

chosen by the Constitution to serve the public interest in securing the production of literary and scientific works of lasting benefit is an independent entrepreneurial approach. You may fail as well as succeed. You may spend ten years writing *Roots* and reap a harvest, or you may spend ten years writing another book and sell three thousand copies. In either event, you must play the rules of the game under the Copyright Act.

This underlying constitutional principle has survived the new law, but there are some new and dangerous implications which have been noted by the Register of Copyrights, the Authors League, and others. The principle of compulsory licensing which had been confined to the recording of music in the 1909 law has been expanded now to cover jukebox use of music, television retransmission of copyrighted television programs, and public broadcasting uses of nondramatic, musical, and graphic works. Accompanying this has been a drastic expansion in the government's role in regulating the uses of copyrighted works. The new Copyright Royalty Tribunal, which has been referred to, will actually be a government price-fixing agency. This burgeoning of government regulation should give no great satisfaction to users or creators, because government regulation does not carry with it a golden guarantee of simplified administration nor the promise of fair and equitable prices. Look at your gas bill and ponder on the value of government regulation.

Has the new act affected the nature of copyright? Like all other property, copyright is a bundle of rights granted by the state either through legislation or court decision. It is only in this sense, true of all property, that copyright is a monopoly. It is not a monopoly in the antitrust sense. As property, copyright was unique under the 1909 act. Other forms of private property impose absolute restraints against public use. A patent, for example, prevents everybody else in the world from using the ideas it protects, even somebody who independently comes upon the same combination of ideas or the same process.

A copyright does not impose these restraints. Anyone is free to use the ideas, or the facts, or the information presented in a copyrighted work. A copyright only

protects the author's expression. Other writers can
draw on those ideas and facts. Other writers are free
to independently create and publish similar, almost
identical, works. The only prohibition copyright imposes is that the next author or the next creator cannot substantially copy the first author's expression.
Copyright under the new law retains that fundamental
nature. The 1976 act does not expand the boundaries of
copyright protection beyond the boundaries of the 1909
act in this essential sense. Under the old law, acquiring a copyright was an automatic process for books and
other library works. One published the book and put a
notice of copyright in it and copyright would automatically adhere. The new law, as Mr. Baumgarten has told
you, applied another automatic method of securing copyright, but it really varies not that much in the essential sense that a government agency does not grant copyright protection and never did. Only the act of Congress
does. The Copyright Office played no role in determining
what works should be copyrighted and what works should
not, except in those instances in which it refused registration, and then as now, that issue will be decided
by the courts in the last analysis.

Copyright does not impose any restriction on the
communication of the information contained in the work
which is protected by the copyright. It was for this
reason, I suppose, that neither the Court of Claims nor
the Supreme Court paid even the slightest attention to
an argument made by the attorney for the National Education Association who decided that he had discovered a
fatal conflict between copyright and the First Amendment. His argument was that the first amendment required
freedom to copy.

No one, no court, has ever decided that freedom of
speech implied the right to get what you read for free.
The Miracle, which was a controversial motion picture
long before the Supreme Court decided *Miller* vs. *California*, was protected by the courts under the First
Amendment. That did not mean that anybody who wanted to
see the movie was now free to go into the theater without buying a ticket. And the same principle applies to
books. Actually, the Copyright Act is probably the only
act of government which provides an underpinning for the

First Amendment, because it provides the financial basis on which authors and publishers can effectively exercise the freedom to write and to publish.

In assessing the implications of the 1976 Copyright
Act for writers, I think it's important to recognize
that the new law is not a windfall measure for those
who create books, plays, and other library works (as we
[the Authors League] told Congress during the hearings).
There has been a lot of misunderstanding about the extent to which the new law varied from the old. As you
look at the two statutes, you do find important sections
of the new Act which are not in the old law. But to a
large extent these focus on such issues as cable television: who shall pay, and how much; or the jukebox
clause; or the changes in the compulsory license provision for recorded music. When one compares the section
in the new Act which prescribes the rights of authors
in their books and plays, one finds that the 1976 law
provides exactly the same rights as those that authors
had under the 1909 act. Composers of music do derive
modest financial benefits from the new law. There is
an increase in the statutory royalty that record companies must pay when they record an author's music. And
there is the jukebox fee which will now be paid and will
probably not be enough to cover the cost of administer-
ing it, let alone paying any of it to the authors. But
the new Act does not increase by one cent the royalties
authors will be able to obtain in contracts for uses of
their literary and dramatic works, and it does not, as
I have said, expand the scope of those basic rights. Indeed, some of our greatest achievements in the Copyright
Revision bill, and we boast a few, are negative. What we
kept out of the Act was almost as important as what we
put into it. These defeated provisions include an exemption for educational copying, a much broader library exemption, and the effort by the public broadcasters to
obtain a compulsory license for the use of literary
works, all of which we successfully opposed.

Of course the 1976 Act has positive implications for
creators of copyrighted works. It does modernize the
1909 law and brings it into line with the laws of other
countries. One of the most important of these provisions
is the establishment of a single term for copyright. It

lasts the life of the author plus fifty years in the
case of works by individual authors, and for 75 years
from publication (or 100 years from creation) for works
of corporate authorship, or other works made for hire.
This change is not one that will reap a financial harvest for most authors. It does not put another nickel
into their pockets during their lifetime. What it does
do is assure that the authors of those comparatively
few works that do survive will, as in Europe, be entitled to protection during their lifetime, and it will
give their families a reasonable period of protection
after their death. Life plus fifty years is not a
drastically new concept. It has been a copyright term
in most European and other countries since the beginning of this century.

Adoption of the single term of copyright makes possible other changes. One, as Mr. Baumgarten explained,
is the elimination of perpetual common law copyright,
thus bringing all works, published and unpublished, into the federal system to be protected only for the term
allowed by the Copyright Act. This is a change of importance to librarians and scholars as well as authors.
Let me illustrate. Three or four years ago, McGraw-Hill
published a biography of Warren Harding by Francis
Russell. It was called *The Shadow of Blooming Grove*, a
book well received by the critics. But it attracted a
good deal of attention for another reason - a strange
quirk in its typography. As the author noted in his pre-
face there was a scattering of blank spaces in the text
of several chapters. For example, on page 345 Russell
wrote, "When Harding delayed his answer, she wrote
again. Finally he replied. . . ." Space, space, space.
Ten lines of broken lines. As Russell explains, the
blank spaces initially had contained excerpts: "I had
quoted from Harding's love letters to Mary Phillips. I
have been forced to make these deletions because of a
restraining order issued by the Court of Common Pleas
in Columbus, Ohio, on a motion by Harding's nephew."

As unpublished writings, the letters were protected
by law, and that protection had no time limit. If they
had been George Washington's unpublished letters, his
living heirs could have enjoined their publication. But
come January 1, 1978, all unpublished writings, books,

letters, diaries, and the like will be protected under
the Copyright Act, not common law. Thus protection will
last for the author's life and 50 years after his or
her death with an outside grace period for works created
before 1978. This means that if in the next century another Mr. Russell wants to quote from the letters of
Jimmy Carter, be they love letters or otherwise, Amy or
her children will not be able to get an injunction in
the Court of Common Pleas of Columbus, Ohio, and prevent the publication of those letters. This whole treas-
ure trove of unpublished resources is opened up for use
after a specified period of time under the new law. But
it's interesting to realize that other inhibitions which
are not copyright inhibitions will still remain to create dilemmas, or, if you will, problems.

Suppose the library or archives holding a valuable
collection refuses access to scholars unless they refrain from quoting or reprinting, even though the authors of the papers has been dead for more than fifty
years, or suppose the library agrees to make the papers
available to an author for quotation or reprinting, but
only on payment of substantial royalties. What we have
to recognize, and it becomes very relevant to this whole
question of copying charges and dissemination of information through the new system, is that the holder who
controls the first copy can still impose conditions -
for example, a private individual or an institution pos-
sessing the first and only copy of Warren Harding's love
letters can accomplish some of the same results (even
though the writing itself has been in the public domain
for two centuries) by simply saying, "I require you to
pay if you want to look at it or if you want to quote
from it." Or suppose the library allows one author or
one historian exclusive access despite the expiration
of copyright protection. In other words, will some libraries, archives, and private holders of collections
employ their physical possession of the papers to
achieve the same results which perpetual common law
copyright permitted or which a limited term of statutory
copyright permitted? And another question, how will the
courts respond to that? Time does not permit an answer.

I will turn now to two specific questions that arise
from Sections 107 and 108 of the Copyright Act - ques-

tions which have engaged authors, educators, librarians, and publishers for a good deal of time in the
last two or three years. They are summarized in that
Senate report which Mr. Brennan mentioned and in Senator McClellan's letter. The Senate report said that
where copying exceeds the limits of Sections 107 and
108, mechanisms should be established or created for
payment; and that where guidelines are needed under
Section 108, they should be developed. Section 107, as
you have been told, simply repeats the criteria of fair
use. The House and Committee reports contain other interesting comments which I will not quote at this point.
These explain that much of the language people have
seized upon as seemingly expanding Section 107 was put
in for cosmetic reasons to satisfy nervous representatives of various constituencies and refer specifically
to the language on photocopying, making the point that
the Congress had not intended to give photocopying special treatment under the doctrine of fair use.

As for guidelines, those that are developed for Section 107 relate to classroom copying of books and periodicals, not to other subjects. They were worked out by
an ad hoc committee of educational organizations representing the National Education Association, the National
Council of Teachers of English, and about thirty other
organizations whose names I don't remember. On our side
of the table were the Association of American Publishers,
some independent publishers represented by one of my
fellow panelists, Mrs. Linden, and the Authors League
of America. One of the reasons we were able to write
these guidelines for educational copying is that we
started with the premise that we were not creating the
Ten Commandments to be carved on Mount Rushmore, there
to endure forever. If we had taken that attitude, we
would have never attempted to make an offer on any aspect of the guidelines for fear we would be writing in
a binding precedent, something that might endure as long
as the new copyright act does. The preamble to the educational guidelines states that the conditions determining the extent of permissible copying for educational
purposes may change in the future, that certain types of
copying permitted under the guidelines may not be permissible in the future, and conversely that in the future

other types of copying not permitted under the guidelines may become permissible. In other words, conditions may change, and we recognized that the guidelines
would have to be adjusted in the future to accommodate
the new circumstances.

The guidelines are available. It would take too much
time to try to detail them, but essentially they establish conditions of brevity, spontaneity, and cumulative
effect. Brevity is defined in terms of word count. One
of the reasons we did that is that brevity, if one attempts to define it linguistically, defies solution.
That *is* a dilemma. But one can adopt word counts or line
counts, recognizing that they do not meet every situation, and also recognizing, as we did, that we were only
stating minimums. There would be situations where fair
use copying would be permitted beyond these guidelines.
What we were doing was saying to everybody involved, "If
you do not go beyond this, there is never going to be a
problem. You may be able to go beyond this, but that may
require consulting with your legal advisor or with someone in your community more familiar with fair use. And
we may indeed even attempt to develop further guidelines."

As far as the author-publisher-library relationship
is concerned, attempts to discuss guidelines were not
fruitful. Some effort was made. The dialogue was interesting, but nonproductive. I did, as Mr. Frase pointed
out, go to CONTU with a series of questions on guidelines. I might also point out that Mr. Frase inadvertently may have left you with the impression that the CONTU
guidelines that were developed (dealing only with the
definition of aggregate quantities for the Section 108 g
clause on interlibrary arrangements) were negotiated by
the publishers and librarians through the good auspices
of CONTU. That is not quite the case. As has been true
all through the revision effort on fair use, library
copying, and public broadcasting, the Authors League
worked with the Association of American Publishers - not
only worked with them but rode on their backs most the
way, in the sense not of their carrying us but of our
driving them. And, as is appropriate, it was the Authors
League, not the publishers, who wrote the letters ob-
jecting to the original CONTU draft guideline in consultation with the AAP and making demands for changes.

The first guidelines were not really all that good
and we reacted rather strongly to them. I say this not
out of pride of authorship, but out of the conviction
that these problems are not publisher-librarian problems. If we only had to deal with the publishers we
would have done much better. They are *author*-publisher-
librarian problems, and we probably take them, in many
instances, far more seriously than the publishers. Indeed, at the very inception of the copyright debate,
one failing of the publishing community was its inabil-
ity to recognize the photocopying problem. It was not
they who recognized it, it was the authors; and it was
only after a period of time that the AAP position
changed, as it became aware of the dimensions of the
problem.

In any event, guidelines probably are required for
several other aspects of Section 108, and what I had
asked the commission was whether they were going to do
anything about this, since they had played a role in
developing the first set of guidelines. We explained
that they ought to tell us, because if they were not,
we would have to consider that factor in planning what
action authors' organizations, librarians' organizations, and publishers' organizations should take. These
are the possible guidelines I ticked off for them:
guidelines defining aggregate quantities for periodical
articles more than five years old, guidelines defining
aggregate quantities and other provisions for in-house
copying, guidelines with respect to 108 g-1, which relates to multiple copying, one at a time or over a period of time. Guidelines spelling out the meaning of
reasonable effort and fair price under the subsection
permitting single copy reproduction to replace lost or
stolen copies. And finally, guidelines relating to reasonable investigation and fair price under the out-of-
print clause which permits a library that has determined
after a reasonable investigation that a copy is not
available at a fair price, to reproduce a copy of the
entire work.

I do feel that these guidelines would not be difficult to prepare. They do not present dilemmas and they
can be drawn probably much more easily than the educational guidelines that were developed. As the ·Authors

League told CONTU last January, we are prepared to work
with the publishers and the library organizations to
formulate the guidelines. We also made other suggestions
to CONTU, including a recommendation that it get to work
on the problem of coin-operated reproduction and come up
with recommendations to Congress for changes in the Act
that would recognize the rights of copyright owners. It
is the mandate of Congress to make such recommendations,
and of course coin-operated reproduction is a problem
that has not been dealt with at all in the new Act, except for the warning provisions that you have been told
about. We also asked CONTU to do what Senator McClellan
had asked them to do, take part in the task of helping
to work out mechanisms for payment. Our requests that
they play a role in this, not necessarily in shaping but
in helping the parties to shape a mechanism, was under-
lined by the March 31 meeting of CONTU at which the
Association of American Publishers unveiled its plan for
a payment center for technical, scientific, and medical
journal articles. The Authors Le.gue did not participate
in the development of this plan and the Authors League
did, promptly upon its presentation to CONTU, arise,
protest vigorously, and announce its opposition for reasons I will mention.

Let me outline the plan in case you are not familiar
with it. What the publishers propose is the establishment of a nonprofit copy payment center. Any journal
publisher can participate in the center. Each publisher
would establish his own copying fees. Beginning with
1978 periodical issues, participating publishers would
print a copying fee on the first page of each article
with a standardized code identifying the article and
thus the publisher. Use of the code would in effect be
a license to copy on payment of those fees to the payment center. Libraries and other users that wish to participate in the center could register, receive an organizational code number, and report their copying and payment fees. Reports of copying could be made in various
ways. For example, an additional copy of the first page
of each article could be marked with the user's code.
This could be done periodically. In other words these
pages could be bundled and sent to the payment center
periodically. Or, the publishers' plan provides that

recording could be done by computerized records of article codes and prices. Payment could be made in one of two ways. It could be accomplished by prepayment: a library exercising its right to copy under the licensing scheme could pay by affixing stamps to the copy of the first page returned to the copying center or use a postage meter to prepay. Or the payment center would collect these reports of copying, prepare billings for participating libraries and other users, and bill periodically for direct payment or for charge against a deposit account.

There is nothing new in the AAP plan. I do not say that critically, I simply state it as a matter of fact. As the publishers' witness acknowledged to the commission last March, all fundamentals of this plan were developed during the 1973 conference between AAP, the Authors League, and the various library organizations in Washington at Dumbarton Oaks. I hate to call it the Dumbarton Oaks Conference because it makes it sound a lot more important than it really was. Nobody set any international monetary standards there. They just sat around and talked about these few elements: the codes for articles and copying fees, an agency to bill and pay, and a guideline to distinguish fair use copying from unfair use copying. That is what we talked about, and we came up with most of these points. Other details were developed in the 1974-75 meetings between library associations, the Authors League, and the AAP. The method of payment by attaching stamps to copies was proposed years ago in a plan published by the Authors League. And prepayment through order forms that are purchased, or through stamps, is used by the British Lending Library.

I should mention that the publishers also raised the question of the possible need for antitrust clearance, which we would oppose under the present structure of the plan. They also said that they might ask Congress to amend Section 108, to deny attorney fees or statutory damages to publishers of technical, scientific, and medical articles who did not join the plan, allowing them only to recover actual damages. That would effectively eliminate copyright protection for such articles, because as a practical matter nobody can afford to sue

for infringement in an area like this for the amount of
money involved, if all they can collect is actual damages.

This bears on one aspect of the copyright bill which
has not been discussed. That is the substantial changes
in the damage provisions which require courts to remit
(i.e., deny) statutory damages in the case of copying
by librarians, educators, or public broadcasters which
they reasonably believed to be fair use, even if it was
not. I should explain that an organization like ASCAP
could never survive if it were only permitted to cover
actual damages from infringement, because the actual
damages may range anywhere from 6 cents to two or three
dollars for an infringement performance. The essence of
enforcement and protection in an area of multiple uses,
each of which is worth very little, is the right of the
copyright owner to recover statutory damages which the
court must fix at a minimum of $250 plus attorney's
fees. The danger of statutory damages against librarians
is eliminated in the area of fair use by the new changes
in the damage provisions.

The Authors League expressed its opposition to the
AAP plan - but not because of the mechanics. Essentially
we think that their combination of the elements that had
already been discussed creates a licensing and payments
mechanism that should work, and can work if it is tried
in good faith.

What we complained about was the fact that the AAP
plan is based on two utterly unacceptable premises.
First that the clearinghouse would be operated solely
by publishers. NEVER! And secondly it was based on the
premise that there would never be any payment to authors
of these articles. Now even if the clearinghouse were
limited to technical, scientific, and medical articles,
that presents a serious problem which we think the AAP
is trying to solve incorrectly. If the clearinghouse is
opened to other articles and materials, and it would be,
then obviously that premise would deny authors of short
stories, poetry, literary articles (and all other works)
the right, which they have under the old copyright law,
to obtain payment for these subsidary uses; payments
which they obtain now in the ordinary course of events.
In many instances, publishers get nothing when the

articles and short stories are reprinted in anthologies. It is the author who gets the whole fee.

As the questioning from CONTU members established, the AAP plan starts with a direct conflict with the copyright act, because under the Copyright Act of 1976, all rights in an article vest in its author. He or she becomes the copyright owner. When asked how they would deal with that problem, AAP explained that all publishers would insist that all authors turn over all rights. We would strenuously fight any clearinghouse that was part and parcel of a plan by publishers of journals to require authors to turn over control of their rights, rights given to them by the Copyright Act. Secondly, the question of payment is distinct from the question of who should run the clearinghouse. As you know ASCAP, which is the major clearinghouse for music, is managed equally by authors and publishers. The sharing of control is a principle we believe any clearinghouse in this field would have to abide by. One additional element that we suggested, and even AAP agreed, is that should users want to be represented in the management of clearinghouses, they or their representatives should be placed on the governing board.

As far as the authors of technical, scientific, and medical articles are concerned, there are two problems. Even assuming that all authors, every author who ever wrote such an article, rejected the idea that he or she ever should be paid a nickel for photocopying - there still remains the question of whether he or she should give up another essential right of authorship which is the right to determine how his or her property should be disposed of. In a new medium, with all of the consequences and implications that this one has, it makes no sense to assume that even authors of this type of material may not want to be paid, and that they want to give over to publishers the governing of this clearinghouse. I don't think they do, and the Authors League doesn't believe they should.

Thus we have the basic problems of control and the structuring of a clearinghouse so that it can accumulate data sufficient to provide for the payment of royalties to authors in those instances where authors wish to receive it. That will include the whole spectrum of authorship, including writers who not only expect to, but would fight for the right to, be paid. Indeed, the big fight would not be whether they should be paid but how much, whether it should be 50 percent or everything.

So that leaves us pretty much in the posture of now waiting for the AAP to change its mind and magnanimously announce that it will indeed work for the establishment of a clearinghouse jointly operated by authors and publishers, and that the clearinghouse will be structured to provide the necessary data that would permit payment to authors as such payments are negotiated.

Time does not permit me to discuss some of the other implications of Sections 107 and 108, but obviously the payments mechanism is one of the most important problems we face and which will have to be dealt with on or before or at least shortly after January 1, 1978. Senator McClellan's warning notwithstanding, I would have to guess it is more likely to be shortly after, than on or before.

DISCUSSION

Herbert S. White: Our invitation to this panel obviously predated the proposal submitted by AAP to CONTU. However the proposal that Mr. Karp talked about will be explained by Mr. Koch.

Elizabeth Smith (Environmental Protection Agency): If the copyright vests in the author, what exactly does the publisher of a journal copyright?

Irwin Karp: Well, the publisher of the journal copyrights the collected work. Also, when he puts his copyright notice on the masthead page, that under the present law and under the new law as well secures copyright for every contribution. Actually, it does not "secure" copyright; under the new law that is already secured. A different situation exists where the material is written by employees of the publisher; that is, where the material is written as a work made for hire. Then the copyright vests in the publisher. But what actually exists under the new law is two different copyrights - a copyright on the periodical as a collective work and a copyright on the individual contributions.

Shirley Jenkins (Science Research Associates): You said that under the new copyright law that the author will carry his own copyright. And I want to know what does the publisher do then? How does he make the registrations, and do we put the author's name on the front of the book and say copyright by the author?

Irwin Karp: No, he doesn't have to. As I explained under the new law, the copyright notice can be in the publisher's name.

Shirley Jenkins: I thought you meant that was just because of several different authors being combined in one publication and that the publisher would copyright the whole work.

Irwin Karp: Under the new law the publisher does not copyright the work, each work. The copyright already exists and it belongs to the author. It exists from the moment the author wrote the article or the monograph or whatever he wrote. And when it's published, that does not change things any. It is just a problem of the new act requiring a notice. And the act does provide that, in the case of a collective work, one notice will suffice, and it could be a notice bearing only the publisher's name. That does not affect ownership of a copyright. It may affect the circumstance in which a user relies on that notice, but that gets too complicated to get into. Each author owns the copyright. He can sell it, if he executes a written agreement transferring the copyright or various of the rights to the publisher; the publisher will then become the owner. One of the things the new law does do is to codify what I think was the law and the House committee report says was the law all along: that the author cannot be presumed to have transferred all of his rights in the copyright simply because he handed a manuscript to a journal for publication. The new law now makes it clear that the author is the original owner of copyright and that when he simply hands the manuscript over for publication, all the journal publisher (and this means any journal publisher, whether it's a popular magazine or a scientific journal) is presumed to have acquired is the right of first publication in that journal and in any subsequent editions of it. Now if there is an express transfer of other rights, then they would go to the publisher as the parties agreed. One of the big problems was that under the present law, there had been a couple of cases in which a presumption was made that because the author delivered the manuscript to the publisher, the publisher had acquired all rights. The new law does not prevent publishers from acquiring rights by express agreement, but there must be express agreements.

Shirley Jenkins: Sorry, I'm going to ask one other question of Mr. Karp. You said that for corporate works, that the statute limitation is 100 years?

Irwin Karp: For works made for hire, the term would be 75 years from publication or 100 years from creation, whichever is shorter. That also would apply to anonymous and pseudonymous works.

Gerald Handfield (Indiana State Library): Early in your talk, you mentioned the fact that the Authors League was, as far as you were concerned, most proud of the negative accomplishments. And one of them was that you opposed, at least this is my understanding, a broader library exemption. I was wondering if you'd explain that.

Irwin Karp: At one point, the proposal was made that there be a library "right" to make a single copy of any article for any user. The exemption would have ended there without a qualification that there could not be systematic copying. In other words, if you did not have Section 108 g in the law, you might read Section 108 d as permitting a library to fill an order for a copy of any article or any other contribution to a journal or collected work for each user who requested it. That would have accomplished what other library proposals had also sought to accomplish and what they thought the fair use doctrine allowed them to do. Anybody who wanted an article

simply could go to a library and the library would
make a copy. That was what the "single copy exemption" was originally proposed to permit. And that
single copy could have been 100,000 copies if 100,000
people each wanted one copy of the article. It was as
simple as that.

Editor's note: Since the presentation of this talk,
the AAP has revised its proposal to include some of the
features requested by Mr. Karp, and the Authors League
now endorses the revised proposal.

BELLA LINDEN

COMMERCIAL PUBLISHERS AND THE NEW COPYRIGHT ACT

In representing the commercial publishers' view, I
believe it appropriate to point out that commercial publishers are not susceptible to being described in a single profile. There are many kinds of commercial functions that are, in the broadest sense, similar. Yet, the
specialized services or functions that each group of
people in each category provide are different and distinct. Therefore their problems are different and distinct. Commercial publishers are publishers of journals
and magazines, and I am clearly distinguishing between
the two generic terms "journal" and "magazine," since
most of us speak of scientific and technical journals
and consider business publications as magazines. Popular publications which appear in serial paperbound form
usually also are deemed magazines rather than journals.
We may refer to what are called trade books, by which
is meant novels, history books, books of poetry, plays,
and so on and so forth. Then there are textbook publishers and reference book publishers, and there are
undoubtedly other categories of publications that I
have failed to mention. Within each of these publishing
categories there are clearly overlaps. They are not
susceptible to precise and absolute definitions that
would result in agreement even by those of us assembled
here as to which publications fall into which category.

Senior Partner, law firm of Linden and Deutsch.

Therefore the issue of what category of work is being
published immediately relates to what the market for
each work is and who its users are likely to be. There
are obviously many overlaps, yet there is usually a distinct community to whom specific publications primarily
are addressed.

Now in addition to recognizing that there are various
kinds of publishing, it is important to reiterate that
publishers by and large do not own printing presses, do
not own binderies, and are not suppliers of paper. Publishers in the private sector today are individuals, organizations, corporations, partnerships; all are entrepreneurs - private-sector entrepreneurs - who primarily
package information for dissemination on paper or via
computerized technology, via microfilm, microfiche, microform, xerography, or whatever other form literary information or knowledge can be transmitted and perceived
by the ultimate user. Therefore the photocopying issue
relates to only one aspect - a temporary aspect - of the
economic enterprise involved in publishing by the so-
called commercial (I prefer to say the private) sector.

I must add here that, as Dr. Lee Burchinal mentioned,
there are government publications which in all essential
respects, including their charges, their advertising,
their marketing facilities and expenditures, are as commercial as the most commercial enterprise I have the
privilege of representing. I particularly call your attention to NTIS which, in addition to requesting copyright protection for government publications and in response to the pressure of the Office of Management and
Budget (OMB) which insists that they must become self-
sufficient, has also engaged in applying for licenses to
private sector publishers for the rights to reprint and
disseminate commercially published works, works produced
in the private sector. They wish to achieve licenses at
what we believe to be extremely modest or low fees or
royalty payments, and they then wish to disseminate and
sell at a profit. To me that is a commercial enterprise
in the most capitalistic sense of the word, not necessarily unjustified but certainly a commercial enterprise.

This is not the proper place to comment on what the
role of government publications really is or what it
ought to be in our society. What I merely wanted to call

to your attention is that the private sector of publishing, which is a commercial sector of publishing, is not the only commercial sector of publishing in the United States.

The role of the publisher really is merely that of a packager. When I say they are packagers, I mean that they are the ones who select what it is they believe ought to be disseminated and addressed to which market, who select which authors, and in which format the package ought to be made for the most appropriate dissemination to meet the demand or possible demand or hoped-for demand of the product. These packagers of information, these commercial publishers, have followed the dialogue and have very actively and vociferously participated in some of the dialogue with respect to the development of the various points of view that have resulted in the copyright law as it has been passed. The commercial publishers look at the law and are pleased that it does have a section of definitions that, in some measure at least, more closely approximate the realities of modern technological methods of fixing information in perceivable form. They look at the law and are pleased that the term of authorship was extended to life plus 50, something they consider to be very worthwhile for only a small segment of authorship. As Mr. Karp has pointed out, very few books, and very little intellectual property does sustain a lifetime plus 50 years of economic and social value sufficient to support any enterprise in any respect whatsoever.

It is interesting that the section in the new law that describes the subject matter of copyright, of what is owned by the copyright proprietor or author, is set forth very modestly yet sufficiently in half a page. The sections and the other related provisions such as national origin and what is a compilation, a derivative work, how that operates, and the role of the U.S. Government are set forth from page 5 to the middle of page 7, about one and one-half pages. Thereafter, the exemptions or limitations on the exclusive rights are set forth between Sections 107 and 118 and are found beginning in the middle of page 7 to the middle of page 31, comprising about 24 pages. That is the basic difference between the Copyright Act of 1909 and the new Copyright Act with respect to the basic rights of the authors and the publishers who were the packagers and, in many instances, the proprietors of the rights through individual authorship or as employees for hire. So that when Mr. Karp says that the role of many publishers' representatives in the Authors League was that of fighting against certain provisions that being the extent of the victory, the statistics I've just quoted simply underline and reinforce the validity of that position.

The question to which I'd like to address myself now is, what interest did you have as users or managers of facilities for users in the rights and in the protection of rights for authors and the private sector of publishers? Should your interests be limited appropriately and properly to taking as many of the rights of publishers and authors away from them in order to facilitate the prompt servicing of users? I submit that I do not believe it appropriate that we be in an adversarial position. I do not believe it less than extremely dangerous to your interests and to the interests of the people you represent and work for, by whom I mean all users of library facilities, all users of intellectual property. If you do not stand alongside us and help us preserve the private sector and help us preserve the competitive entrepreneurial rights of authors to find publishers who will publish their works, you will be subject to a monolithic, possibly government-sponsored publishing industry. The private sector cannot survive in the face of the new technology and the ease of using intellectual properties without payment and without authority, unless you participate in the forefront with those defending the multiauthor, multipublisher system of creation and dissemination of intellectual property that is the essence of this country's freedom of intellectual creation and freedom of thought and freedom of expression.

The publishers direct the work of authorship. They package it for a specific market and unless they believe that the market exists, unless they believe there is a market for a competitive work, unless they believe there are users who are willing and able to pay for the competitive work, they cannot and will not publish it. That is not to say that intellectual property will dry up overnight, and that is not to say that intellectual prop-

erty will disappear from this country. We have seen what
happens in some other countries with socialist systems
where intellectual property is sponsored. Where you have
a monolithic single bureaucratic system of sponsorship
of intellectual property, you do not, I must emphasize,
you do not get divergent views expressed as you do in
our society. You do not get the intellectual foment and
the resulting creativity on which our nation is based
and under which it has prospered. I'm saying this to you
even though I'm sure you all know it, but I'm repeating
it today within the context of the library photocopying
issue, within the context of the issue that is just a
short distance away, and that is the computerized, technological uses of intellectual property. I'm saying this
to you because I believe it is your responsibility, I
reiterate, your responsibility, as much as it is the responsibility of the authors and the private sector of
publishing to preserve or, what is even more important
immediately, to prevent the eroding of an on-going system of creativity and packaging of intellectual property
which you utilize in your everyday lives and your professional functioning and in your leisure time.

I am not suggesting, as Chicken Little did, that the
sky is falling. The sky will not fall today. The sky
will not fall tomorrow. However, if the erosion of the
market for private intellectual property continues,
eventually the sky will fall, and by that time it will
be too late. You cannot recreate a system of private
entrepreneurial authorship and private-sector publishing
overnight or even within a decade or two after it has
been destroyed. Wherever a vacuum exists, that vacuum
will be filled, but it will be filled by a monolithic
bureaucracy and a single publishing organization. I can
tell you that authorship in the USSR is much more limited than it is here and has no rights whatsoever outside
the VAP organization at this time. This has happened not
only because the USSR is a communist state, it happened
simply because whenever there isn't any competition,
with different points of view and different expressions,
you end up with that kind of simplistic, deadly bureaucracy.

As for photocopying, we will have clearinghouses,
certainly more than one clearinghouse. I too objected to

the AAP clearinghouse when it was announced at the CONTU meeting. Like Irwin Karp, I did not have the privilege of participating in its drafting. I believe that authors and private-sector publishers are partners in the creation and dissemination of intellectual property in this country, and I believe that the more of them there are, the better it is for you and me and for future generations. I cannot conceive the existence of any rights in intellectual property where the author is excluded from the management of that property, unless the author has sold the rights to a specific property to an individual publisher. The division of labor and partnership I suggested earlier includes you and I don't mean only those of you who are present. I look at you as representative of the community which is interested in the dissemination of the intellectual property that the authors create and that the publishers package and distribute. Even though capital investment in hardware is valuable and important and should and will go on, the hardware is no different than trains or aeroplanes. Without passengers, they are not needed. Without authorship, without intellectual property packaged by publishers, your multimillion or multibillion dollar expenditure in the most efficient rapid servicing of users of intellectual property will inexorably be a failure if you do not support the rights of authorship and publishing and insist that they remain vigorously alive as part of this country's private sector.

It is inevitable that there will be a clearinghouse or there will be clearinghouses. When is only a question of time. However, if you are so impatient that you must have any intellectual property immediately, free, gratis, without authorization, and if you are able to achieve that, I am convinced that you will live to regret that achievement: at least the next generation will live to regret it. But if you can accept some inconveniences while you're waiting for the development of this marvelous hardware or these systems you're setting up to service users and intellectual property, if you are impatient and get clearinghouse rights initially imperfectly, perhaps always imperfectly, but each year in a better format from a more efficient organization, as publishers and authors become accustomed to the new technology, we

can all go down the road in peace together, all of us
functioning in our appropriate division of labor. It
will take all of us functioning appropriately to preserve the multiplicity of creativity by authors, the
multiplicity of entrepreneurial efforts by the hundreds
and hundreds and perhaps thousands of publishers of the
various kinds of publications that are produced in the
private sector. And your function and your efforts will
appropriately be the servicing to the users of all of
that intellectual property without stifling it, without
eroding it, by insisting that you wanted it all yesterday.

A clearinghouse initially has to be a modest testing
enterprise, because it is a prospective effort that cannot be encased in bronze in the law because the law historically and practically is a retrospective exercise.
First we experience an event, then we legislate, and
then we make more mistakes than not, with respect to an
event that has already occurred. Well, we are talking
about prospective uses. We ought to have clearinghouses,
perhaps initially with a three-year agreement or a five-
year agreement, certainly not longer, and then take a
good hard look at what we have accomplished. We ought to
start initially with areas of photocopying that are susceptible to easier management in the clearinghouses. We
ought to recognize that the clearinghouse itself is a
profile, a beginning, a microcosm of what we all intend
to accomplish.

Now I speak on behalf of the publishers in the private, commercial sector. We recognize the new technological uses and methods of dissemination used in servicing
information users. We want to be alive and be profitable.
You can make this possible. We will fight in any event
to survive, and it is not only appropriate, but I believe it is your duty and obligation to fight alongside
us with patience and with strength so that we do retain
the kind of intellectual freedom and intellectual and
creative achievement in this country that has been our
history and will continue to be.

DISCUSSION

John Donnell (Indiana University): I'm a teacher rather than a librarian, but I think that I would probably be speaking for some of the librarians also.
Could Mrs. Linden and Mr. Karp perhaps indicate to
us what procedures and practices are to be used in
Bloomington, Indiana, and in other university communities. How should they be different, beginning
the first of January, than they are or have been in
the last three years? I'm particularly interested
from the standpoint of the teacher, but I assume the
librarians would be interested in those kinds of
things, too. I assume the law does make some changes,
as Mr. Karp and some of the other speakers indicated,
in that it doesn't state that fair use is only a re-
petition of the law as it existed. There are some
specific changes for librarians, but there's been
outrageous photocopying by faculty members. I assume
that publishers and authors suspect something different is about to happen. What will be different?

Bella Linden: We expect to have a clearinghouse by then,
or at least the beginnings of a clearinghouse, and we
expect to be down the road to resolving this problem.
We don't expect perfection by January 1, 1978. There
will be casualties along the way. What we are saying
is, that even Section 107, the fair use section,
which really means do unto others as you would have
them do unto you, is sufficiently clear so that all
of you and all of us know when you are really hurting
by photocopying more than you ought. You can, in the
meantime, seek permission from publishers. You won't
always get it. You can seek permission from authors.
You won't always get it. But you don't always get
everything you seek in any other area of your life.
Perhaps some of you do, but I'm a little more pessimistic about that and don't expect to get everything
all at once. We should, by January 1, 1978, start to
function as a team, you and I and Irwin and the rest
of us. That's all we can hope for. That's a beginning,
and with time, as long as we're a team and working together, the long-term results will be worthwhile for

all. Publishers and authors can't make money on a clearinghouse in the first year, or even the first five years of its existence. They consider it fire insurance. You buy fire insurance in case the house burns down. You don't need to invest to spend it. The clearinghouse is an investment against increased photocopying, the increased ease and less costly photocopying that's not only on the rise, but which exists today and will continue to become more effective and more efficient. We're starting. Let us start together, and we will survive together.

Irwin Karp: I'll just come back to classroom copying for a minute, which I think was part of the question you were asking. The problem is illustrated by that sign in a copying mill near an eastern university I visited recently which said; "This is a chance to do all your publishing quickly and never be turned down. Make up your curriculum for the year. Send your students over here and we'll run it all for three cents a page." Well, that is obviously infringement. It always has been. It always will be. And that I do not think is as much a teacher problem as it is a publisher-author problem. The explanation of the copyright law to the copying mills surrounding that campus and other campuses may not work. I saw an example of a more aggressive solicitation of business in a university area in California. Some mills may have to be sued, but you and I are not talking about copying mills.

As far as copying through libraries or other institutional facilities is concerned, the first step would be the guidelines I mentioned, which are explicit guidelines. One of the problems is that as soon as the new copyright bill was passed we suggested to the Ad Hoc Committee that we sit down and prepare some sort of formal explanation for the educational community. They have had an exercise of their own and have thus far done a little. They said they would get back to us, and I think it's up to us now to remind them that questions like yours are being asked. We hesitated for a while to take it upon ourselves to start preaching to teachers, because that's partly a function of the Ad Hoc Group which represents a spectrum of patrons.

But the publication of the guidelines itself will help quite a bit. As far as putting together custom- ized anthologies is concerned, I think it would be helpful if more publicity were given to operations that have gone on for years, where that very type of mass copying has been done under authorization. It is not a question of speculating about a clearinghouse. So it is a combination of the guidelines which permit a modest amount of copying to be done during the course, and permission through other means for the larger scale copying that's really publishing.

Sheri Masiakowski (St. Anthony of Padua Parish, Milwau- kee): I represent a religious institution involved in making multiple copies for nonprofit use, and I have two questions. First, is there any provision for nonprofit religious organizations as far as the copy- right procedures go? And second, I think I've heard more than rumor regarding a clearinghouse for sacred music publication? Do you have any information on either of these?

Irwin Karp: There is no nonprofit exemption for copying by religious or any other organization in the copy- right law.

Bella Linden: May I point out that there are, well I can think of one right this minute in New York, Ceber Crest. That's a religious publishing house. Do you want it to go out of existence? Do you want it all for free?

Sheri Masiakowski: No, I'm wondering if there is some kind of equalization or clearing center. Specifically, we're involved in putting together a hymnal, let's say 1,000 or 2,000 copies of something that will not be copyrighted, but will include songs from a number of different publishers. There had been talk of a clearinghouse where we might write to obtain permis- sion from a number of different places. Is there any implementation of that going on at present?

Bella Linden: May I tell you that I represent music pub- lishers as well, and my clients put out books, music songbooks, etc., not only of their own publications,

but of other publishers. They write for permission,
and they publish. It's done all the time. There are
thousands and thousands of publications of collections of works that are not from one publisher.
There's never been any problem to my knowledge, except for perhaps the one occasional song, so that it
doesn't seem to be a pressing need.

Sheri Masiakowski: I've heard a great deal about it. I
just finished legalizing one hymnal in New Jersey and
working on another one from scratch and I have heard
rumors to the effect that something like that might
be going on. I know that there is a company in Arizo-
na that serves as sort of a clearinghouse, but it
does not take care of writing for permissions.

Bella Linden: Well, there may be somebody who's interested in doing that kind of work, and that's all
right as long as the composer gets paid or agrees to
give it without pay.

Ruth Jackson (Virginia State College): Before coming to
this conference I thought I understood to some extent
the implication for making live recordings, but after
listening to some of the presentation, some of my un-
derstandings have been destroyed. Would you clarify
three questions for me? First, when is it that a non-
creation becomes a copyrighted work? Second, if a live
performance is being recorded by a person and it is
also being recorded simultaneously by a producer, is
the former in violation of the new copyright law? And
third, when one is involved with copyrighted material
how can one be sure that a live performance is now
copyrighted when the whole of production and dissemination methodology is so much more nebulous than when
one is dealing with printed material? How can one always afford to wait and say "I will check on this? I
will try to find out if it will be available at a lat
er time?"

Irwin Karp: Well, let me try to clarify this. Are you
asking if you walked into a Broadway theater with a
tape recorder and recorded a performance of *Equus*
would you be infringing copyright?

Ruth Jackson: Well, not necessarily Broadway. It could be an outdoor performance.

Irwin Karp: Well, let's take a regional theater.

Ruth Jackson: All right. Yes.

Irwin Karp: That's an infringement.

Ruth Jackson: Number two. The second question was when is it that a nonprint creation becomes a copyrighted work?

Irwin Karp: Well, under the present law, *Equus* doesn't even have to be copyrighted. A play, even though it has never been copyrighted, is protected under common law against unauthorized recording. Against anything. *Equus* became copyrighted when it was published or previously registered in the Copyright Office, which I presume they have done by now. Under the new law, if it were a newly written play, it would be copyrighted, it would become copyrighted when the author wrote it on a piece of paper.

Ruth Jackson: All right. That's written on a piece of paper. My question really pertains to those things not written on a piece of paper. This is why I find it difficult to understand.

Irwin Karp: All right. As Mr. Baumgarten explained, any work under the new law becomes copyrighted as soon as it's created and recorded in some tangible form, whether it's written on paper or recorded on tape. Before that it's still going to be protected under common law. That's the one area where common law will continue. The answer is that you assume, as they do in the rest of the world, in any country that has a copyright law, that most things you hear on the air or see in the theater are copyrighted. If you're anxious to record it, the burden is on you to go make sure it isn't copyrighted before you go to record it. That's the way it works all over the world. It's worked that way for a hundred years. And it really has worked that way in this country.

Ruth Jackson: All right. You've answered my question. What you are saying is that one really cannot do live recording legally. Not really.

Bella Linden: May I say something? The one thing that has always disturbed me is when the copyright law says that something is the right of the authors and you have to get permission, people assume that you can't do it, or you can't do it legally. The fact is, you can do it and you can do it legally. You ask permission. You pay a fee as the fee is called for, just as you are barred from going into a commercial theater upon refusing to pay. You have to pay or they have to agree to let you in for nothing, but that doesn't mean that it is illegal or unavailable to you. Like the clothing you buy, like the paper you're holding, it's all available to you in this country at a price and if you're prepared to pay the price, you get it. The same is true of intellectual property that is created and owned by the copyright proprietor.

Richard De Gennaro (University of Pennsylvania): I don't have a question, but I do have a comment that I do feel moved to make. I'd just like to remind the publishers that we librarians in the audience are customers as well as copyright infringers. Last year my library bought $1.3 million worth of the products of the authors and the publishing industry. Many of these would never have been published had it not been for the library market. I feel that the libraries are doing their share to preserve the free enterprise system and the American way of life.

Bella Linden: You're absolutely right. If I did not believe that, I would not have made the comments that I did. You bought $1.3 million of publications?

Richard De Gennaro: Actually we didn't do it. The taxpayers did.

Bella Linden: The taxpayers. All right. You bought $1.3 million of publications. Are you prepared to respond as to whether you would have bought $1.3 million if you could have gotten $1.2 million for free of the $1.3 million? That's what hurts the publishers and the authors. And that's what fair use says, and that's what Section 108 is all about, and that's what the Congressional report is all about. If you want to buy hardware and photocopy the material instead of buying it, you won't be buying it. What we are saying to you is that if you want to photocopy it instead of buying it, give us our fair share. Don't give it all to the hardware manufacturers. That's all we're saying. Let us survive also.

HOW THE PROFESSIONAL SOCIETY AS PUBLISHER VIEWS THE NEW COPYRIGHT ACT

WILLIAM KOCH

Introduction. How do publishers view the new copyright law? While I cannot speak for the publishing community as a whole, nor even for other large not-for-profit journal publishers, I am confident that the American Institute of Physics is not alone in looking forward positively to the implementation of the new copyright law in 1978. In our view, the new law not only provides reasonable protection for the professional rights of authors and the financial obligations of publishers, it also will encourage the application of new technology to a range of new uses of copyrighted material. I certainly expect the new law to strengthen our ability to promote the chartered purpose of the American Institute of Physics, which is the advancement and diffusion of the knowledge of physics and its application to human welfare.

Let me begin by giving you a brief sketch of how AIP presently accomplishes its purpose. I shall then discuss how the new copyright law applies to scientific society publishers in general and to AIP in particular. Following this, I shall refer to the specific procedures that were developed by the Governing Board of the American Institute of Physics at its meeting on 2 April 1977.

Director of Publications, American Institute of Physics; President-elect, National Federation of Abstracting and Indexing Services.

Next I shall make a few remarks about how we are co-
operating with other publishers to establish the new
copyright regime intended by Congress. I shall conclude
with the vexing question of abstracts: How does the new
law apply to abstracts, excerpts, or summaries of articles?

AIP as a journal publisher. The American Institute
of Physics and its nine member societies publish over
100,000 pages per year in original and translated journals devoted to research and education in physics and
astronomy. These pages represent a financial investment
to physics and astronomy societies of about $10 million
per year. They also constitute a comprehensive archive
of the scientific and professional output of the physics
and astronomy community in the United States. Included
in these pages is almost 90 percent of what is published
in the United States in physics and astronomy research
and education, as well as translations of the most important 50 percent of the physics and astronomy research
published in Russian in the USSR.

This publishing program has had a long and successful
history because it has maintained high scientific standards while keeping subscription rates low. The prices
paid by libraries for AIP journals are two to five times
lower than those paid for other privately published physics and astronomy journals, when measured in dollars per
word or per standard page, and consequently the circulation figures for AIP journals are several times larger.
Furthermore, the permissions policies of AIP and its member societies are liberal, in order to encourage fair
use photocopying and other forms of republishing. It is
our intent to continue these policies and to encourage
wide dissemination of the physics and astronomy literature under the new law.

*General comments on society journals and the new copy-
right law.* The new copyright law has been called an "author's law." Obviously, one of its principal purposes is
to encourage the creativity of authors by strengthening
the protection of their intellectual and property rights.
But to me a remarkable aspect of the new law is that it
apparently also will be successful in protecting the interests of scientific societies as publishers of collections of individually authored research articles in the

form of journals. To see how this may be accomplished, let us consider first how such journals are actually produced and disseminated.

Historically, the process begins when a group of scientists defines and identifies itself by forming a scientific society devoted, typically, to a narrow subdiscipline of a scientific field. The creation of a new journal is often the main motivation. As potential authors, these scientists have thereby collectively undertaken to develop and improve scientific standards within their subdiscipline. Following well-established models, they agree voluntarily to submit their future articles to review by their peers and to participate in the operation of this peer review process. They do not expect to be paid for writing articles by the journal publisher, which is, after all, their own society. Indeed, under the page charge system, the authors arrange to contribute funds to the publisher rather than the reverse, as in the case of authors of commercial books. Page charges help to keep down subscription prices and therefore increase circulation, which, in turn, promotes the interests of the authors as scientists and the scientific standing of their subdiscipline. In return for their professional services in this collective endeavor, the members of a scientific society can usually get a subscription to their journal at a low incremental run-off cost, often as part of their society dues.

In this relatively simple noncommercial environment, scientific societies as publishers have traditionally not been much concerned with copyright. Usually it is assumed, with varying degrees of formality, that the process of peer review and eventual acceptance for publication, which every article in a journal issue must undergo, is sufficient to give the society the right to the copyright of the issue and each of its articles. In a very real sense the authors collectively *are* the society, so it is perfectly natural for the society to represent the authors' interests in marketing, sales, permissions, and other aspects of the journal dissemination process.

In the future, and the future is already upon us, the journal publishing process will be more complex because of an emormous expansion in the range of technological options available for information dissemination. The future looks bright for society publishers, if they can take full advantage of this technology. Here is the great merit of the new copyright law: it will permit a scientific society to continue to represent and serve its members, and to benefit society at large, provided only that the individual author formally transfers his or her copyright to the society.

Let us look at some of the new dissemination options. Not only will journal issues continue to be handled as collections of articles, but single articles will be available from the original publisher as well as from republishers. Formats will expand to include microform editions of articles and journals and computerized editions of journals. Within the next two years the American Institute of Physics will, for example, have the full text of all its journal articles available in computer-readable form, for the production of assorted collections of articles and derivatives, such as computer tapes of author-prepared abstracts and journal indexes.

One significant aspect of these developments is that the various formats will also be available simultaneously, relatively promptly, and economically. Most existing computer tapes of abstracts are useless for purposes of current awareness, since the abstracts on them typically refer to articles published four to six months previously. In contrast, some of AIP's tapes are already today available even before the journals themselves are printed. Another significant point is that computerized typesetting is now becoming more economical than even the low cost typewriter composition methods pioneered by AIP and its member societies.

Scientists as authors will, of course, have the option to retain their copyrights and to disseminate their articles without benefit of independent peer review, or they can elect to transfer their rights and request the scientific society as publisher to act in their behalf in reviewing, editing, and disseminating their articles. The result for the author in using the society publisher should be an article that is economically and speedily produced and widely and accurately disseminated.

The new law has the following features which will be particularly important to scientific society publishers:

1. An author establishes copyright in his own name at time of creation of the manuscript of an article.
2. The copyright owner has the right to control the production and marketing of the copyrighted work and of its derivatives, such as abstracts.
3. A valid transfer of copyright from the author to the society must be made formally in writing.
4. The copyright of a collection of articles in a journal issue protects not only the collection but each individual article in the collection. Nevertheless, the inclusion of a copyright notice on each article will clarify whether the publisher or the author is the copyright owner.
5. The notice of copyright must appear on each photocopy of an article made by a library, archive, or other reprint center.
6. Photocopying by a library or archive which is part of an institution operated for commercial advantage is subject to greater restrictions than photocopying by a nonprofit institution.

Scientific societies will have to recognize these features and take them into account in establishing appropriate procedures for encouraging the continuation of both "fair use" photocopying without fee *and* "beyond fair use" photocopying for a fee by libraries as well as by authorized reprint and computer-tape service centers.

AIP policies under the new law. The policies of the American Institute of Physics are still under development, but will be implemented before the end of the year to accord with the new law in 1978. The approvals obtained to date from our governing board already provide a framework for the policies to come. The most important single element in the policy is the intent to establish a valid copyright in the name of the journal owner not only for the collective work (the journal issue) but also for each contribution to that work (the journal article).

Our board members have agreed that AIP and its member societies must obtain the copyright to each journal article, so that the publisher can negotiate uniformly and effectively with republishers and other users of journals in the best interests of the member scientific soci-

eties and of the individual physicists and astronomers
as authors. For example, it would be unreasonable to
expect the publisher to consult individual authors each
time a new contractor wants to start a photocopying,
translating, information disseminating, or other republishing service based on the journals. AIP's policy is
to encourage the widest possible dissemination of research results. This is central to our service role in
the physics-astronomy community. But it can only be done
if the procedures involved are simple and uniformly the
same from article to article and from journal to journal.

The procedures whereby AIP will establish definite
copyright to each article are basically two in number:
first, the opening page of each article will have the
prescribed copyright notice giving the name of the copyright owner (AIP or one of its member societies, if the
societies adopt the same procedures they have approved
for AIP), along with such other items as will define the
article citation and the article copying fee expected
from the republisher. Second, each author will be requested to transfer in writing whatever copyright is
legally transferable, even when the author is a U.S. government employee, but the transfer will be limited by
certain rights to be reserved for authors. Thus transfer
of copyright is to become part of the process of submit-
ting a manuscript for publication. Such a transfer has
been accepted practice in the past for some journals,
among which are those of the American Chemical Society,
and will become accepted and straightforward now for
most authors in our journals. To provide additional protection for the interests of authors, the governing
board intends to develop a list of reasonable rights to
be reserved by authors for their use of their own published material.

The principal author group that may require exceptional treatment is U.S. government employees. There is
no question that a research report written by a scien-
tist employed by the U.S. government as part of his or
her official duties is in the public domain and is not
copyrightable. However, there are two situations which
make an article derived from a "public-domain" report
copyrightable. First, the writer may create a derivative

work outside of his/her official duties on his/her own time. The author then owns the copyright to this derivative work, and may transfer that copyright to the publisher of the derivative work, even though the report from which it is derived is still in the public domain. Second, a journal publisher who, as a result of peer review, makes changes in the original work, with the author's approval, makes a derivative work, the copyright in which vests directly in him/her.

A careful observant of this proposed procedure will immediately ask whether, if the U.S. government provides page-charge funds to AIP, AIP should be considered as a contractor commissioned by the government to put the original work in publishable form, in which case the copyrightability would be in question.

We do not agree that that result would accord with the facts. The page charges established by AIP and its member societies to cover the prerun costs of producing the pages of the journal article are a nonobligatory contribution. Indeed, a U.S. government author can have his/her article published even if he/she does not pay the page charge if the journal editor accepts the article based on scientific merit alone. Thus there would be no factual basis for a conclusion that AIP was either retained or commissioned by the U.S. government.

There may arise exceptional situations where the U.S. government will want to pay the prerun costs as well as the printing and mailing costs (i.e., runoff costs) of publishing an article. In this case, AIP would consider making an agreement with the government under which AIP would retain copyright in its own name for a specified number of years and thereafter assign the copyright to the U.S. government.

The detailed position to be taken vis-à-vis the U.S. government employees is still to be developed by the AIP Governing Board for its journals. It is expected that the position may want to be developed cooperatively with other publishers and the Federal Council for Science and Technology. Nevertheless, the considerations described herein are a demonstration of the value society publishers see in the greater specificity of the new copyright law and its greater applicability to present-day situations compared to the old law. It will now be possible

to respond to the intent of Congress in our rapidly
changing technological environment.

Participation with other publishers. The new copyright law establishes principles that are intended to
apply to all. In order to be consistent with this intent of Congress, AIP and other society publishers of
technical, scientific, and medical journals are participating with other publishers and republishers in the
design and development of a "copy payments center" concept developed by a task group of the Association of
American Publishers. This center will collect from the
user and distribute to the publisher the fees prescribed
by the individual publisher for the copying of articles
appearing in the publisher's journal. Once the charter
of the center has received appropriate clearances from
the Justice Department Anti-Trust Division and the center becomes incorporated as a not-for-profit membership
corporation, AIP will consider becoming a member publisher. Such participation is made possible by the AIP
Governing Board's adoption of the procedures for the
limited transfer of authors' copyrights to the publisher
I have already described.

Treatment of author-prepared abstracts. Scientific
society publishers are accountable to their memberships
for the use to which the material in their journals is
put, and for the accuracy and promptness with which it
is disseminated. This includes excerpts, abstracts, and
derivative works of all kinds.

Primary journal publishers have always respected each
other's copyrights to parts of articles by, for example,
asking permission of each other to reprint a graph or a
table from a previously published article. The American
Institute of Physics and its member societies require
anyone who wishes to reprint a figure or other excerpt
from an article to obtain also the author's permission;
and we will continue this policy under the new law, as
a matter of intellectual courtesy to the original author.

There are many publishers of secondary information
from journal articles presently freely copying or deriv-
ing abstracts from the primary journals who will now be
required to obtain permission to do this from the copyright holder, i.e., the primary journal publisher. But
the primary journal publisher will not necessarily grant

a free license to reprint abstracts to a secondary
service. Increasingly, abstracting and indexing services
will want to offer not only printed collections of abstracts or other excerpts, but also computer tapes of
abstracts and on-line computer searches of such data
bases. Combined with single-article reprinting such
services could, in principle, have a profound effect
on the economics of primary journal distribution. Aside
from economics, another effect on the primary journal
publisher of copying or rewriting abstracts is the introduction and propagation of errors. At the same time,
primary journal publishers themselves are computerizing
the journal production process and are increasingly
able to provide a machine-readable version of their abstracts or even of whole articles. For these reasons it
is clear that primary journal publishers will take full
advantage of all their rights under copyright to exercise control over the systematic use by others not only
of whole articles but of parts of articles such as abstracts.

In the case of the American Institute of Physics,
our policies in this area will undoubtedly be guided by
the following principles:

1. Secondary information services wanting to copy
   AIP abstracts or to write abstracts of AIP articles, or, in general, wanting to create a data
   base of items which can stand for AIP journal articles, will have to negotiate a licensing agreement with AIP. This must include specification of
   all products or services which will use these abstracts or items, so that their potential impact
   on AIP primary journals can be determined.
2. A free license will be granted if this potential
   impact is likely to be negligible; for instance,
   if the proposed services are designed for a market which does not overlap with the market for
   AIP's own services and journals. Otherwise an appropriate charge will be made.

Probably the more important issue with respect to abstracts is the copyrightability of a computer tape of
abstracts. Such tapes are now commonplace and are the

first stage, as I have already indicated is the situation at AIP, to computer tapes of the complete journal.
It is our position that both the tapes of abstracts and
of journals must be protected by copyright just as are
the printed abstracts and journals. Presumably such protection is to be provided at the input of a computer
system and will result in licensing arrangements as
there are copyright protection and licensing arrangements for the use of the printed journals in any marketing and distribution system.

   Conclusion. We are impressed by the cooperation all
sectors of the publishing community are evidencing in
the desire to implement the new law, by the encouragement of prestigious bodies such as the National Commission of Libraries and Information Science and the Commission on New Technological Uses of Copyrighted Works,
and by the soundness of the new copyright law to which
so many contributed. The future looks bright both for
the implementation of *new* technologies to meet the complex information needs of our society, and for the preservation of what is best in traditional practices.

DISCUSSION

Elizabeth Smith: In regard to author-prepared abstracts,
   is the practice of NLM of picking up the author-prepared abstracts for *Index Medicus* contrary to the new
   copyright law in your view?

William Koch: There are very few of the secondary publishers, including the National Library of Medicine,
   that have arrangements with primary publishers and
   that do indeed recognize the copyright. In the case
   of NLM, they do have an arrangement for licensing the
   use as they obtain a license from Chemical Abstract
   Service for the use of their tape, so there they are
   recognizing or paying for the rights to use the material copyrighted by *Chemical Abstracts*. *Chemical Abstracts*, on the other hand, has freely copied and
   freely rewritten many of the abstracts that appear

in the primary journal, so part of the answer to
your question is that NLM, because of the specific
arrangement with *Chemical Abstracts,* does recognize
certain abstracts, but by and large it is not recognizing other copyrights. Now we at the American Institute of Physics have a contractual arrangement
with Energy Research and Development Agency (ERDA),
and ERDA is also being licensed to use our material.
We are supplying that material, and the system works
beautifully, so we are going to try to stimulate
more discussions to see how more uses of primary publisher tapes of abstracts and secondary publisher
tapes of abstracts can be made, and that copyright
recognition is carried on straight through.

Steven Falk (University of Missouri, St. Louis): First
I'd like to thank Mr. Koch for giving a talk which
made me feel better in what I think has been a most
trying and vexing afternoon. Secondly, I'd like to
ask both Mr. Koch and Mr. Karp to go back to the
point requiring authors to transfer copyrights to the
journal. In physics, especially, do you think there's
going to be a problem of freedom of speech or freedom
of press violation if an author says "I don't want to
turn over my copyright permission"? In physics your
organization controls, as you say, 90 percent of all
publications. I wonder if you foresee any legal problems which may spill over into other journals.

William Koch: We don't see any legal problems. The procedure has been approved by the governing board, and
let me say to you that the governing board is made up
of authors and is under the control of authors. If it
finds that the procedures are not appropriate and are
not being implemented so as to protect authors'
rights, that governing board and those authors are
going to change that procedure. That is the value of
the system that we have, so I don't have any concern
that we're not going to be always consistent with
what our authors want us to do. They control us.

Steven Falk: Then to Mr. Karp. Do you foresee commercial
publishers and journals having that same sort of requirement, and would authors stand for that?

Irwin Karp: Some commercial journal publishers do do
that. Just an example of why it's not quite as simple
as doing it or not doing it, I don't see any reasons
why the author of an article to be published in a
physics journal has to turn over the copyright. With
all due respect to the AIP, that's nonsense. One of
the great new changes in the copyright law is to recognize that copyright is divisible. Actually, that's
something courts had already declared under the 1909
act. In fact the Authors League happened to have won
the case in which that judicial decision was handed
down. Divisible copyright simply means that each of
the uses of a work is protected by accepted rights.
All I require is transfer of those particular rights
that would be exercised: photocopying, abstracting,
or translation, for example. Each is a separate right.
Secondly, to illustrate, I couldn't for the life of
me see why, for example, AIP would require Professor
Smith to turn over the motion picture rights in his
article. No one is going to use them anyway, but what
is AIP going to do with them? Or why would authors
have to turn over the television rights? One can
transfer rights under the new law for a year, five
years, or forever. Now the journals and the authors
of technical articles and journals might well consider if they really thought about it, and I know
they have, that it may be one thing to turn over the
photocopying rights to ease the administration, or
to just grant the photocopying rights to the clearinghouse, but why should I turn over to AIP for the life
of my copyright, which is my life plus 50 years, the
right to reprint my article in, for example, a book
of my writings? That is one of the rights the author
will reserve. I think that's one of the ones. In
other words, there's a collection of rights to be
transferred, some may be and some not. So this blanket policy requires a good deal more examination and
could have quite different results than the broad approach that's been described so far. However, I don't
see freedom of speech as an issue.

Ben Weil (temporarily with AAP/TSM Copy Payment Center:
I'm on a six-month loan assignment, if you know what

that means. I feel somewhat like the gentleman in the circus who stands behind the tree, usually with his head showing and has baseballs thrown at him. In this case I think that my head hasn't even been showing, but I think it's only fair to talk a little about the copy payment center that a group of publishers both within and outside the AAP, and also jointly with the Information Industry Association, has set up, and why it is being talked about. First of all, with the copyright law's imminent implementation at the end of this year, if there is no mechanism in place for copying which goes beyond fair use in the CONTU guidelines, said copying would be illegal, and in organizations such as my regular employer, our legal counsel has told us that we must shut down. This goes against the dictum in Senator McClellan's report in which he said that he wishes mechanisms to be developed to permit copying that is not permitted by the new copyright law.

Now it is perfectly true that it would be possible for libraries in the private sector or in any sector to negotiate or attempt to negotiate licenses with publishers to permit photocopying. This would require some hundreds of libraries to negotiate with some hundreds of publishers, with consequent dislocations of all concerned. At least the publishers I've talked to, in the main, have not exactly solicited that type of business, so that it has seemed to be desirable to initiate what has long been discussed, which is the concept of a central operation. I'm not calling it a clearinghouse, because this mechanism, and Irwin Karp described it very accurately, is not a clearinghouse. It does not attempt to provide on behalf of the publishers anything other than, through the system, the right to make copies if you pay the fees that the publisher has put on his copying. But the groups that have been involved in this are a good many of the for-profit publishers and also a great many of the not-for-profit publishers. For example, the Council of Engineering and Scientific Society Executives, known as CESSE, which publishes something over 200 journals in the scientific not-for-profit field, has given it its support to and is represented on the committee that is designing this system.

We haven't yet gotten together a list of the journals that will be in the system. This is very early in the game, but a rough estimate indicates the majority of the top 600 or 700 journals will be in this system if nothing stops it. We are trying to believe that the system can be developed in a manner which will not have some of the objections that you've heard today. The system does recognize a good bit of the facts of life. It does not intend in any way to block out copying of fair use under the CONTU guidelines, but only to provide a mechanism for that kind of copying which is in excess of them. It is a system for which we're at present detailing the operating system. We're intending to solicit and to continue to solicit comments from the various communities involved. There are admittedly in this field many complications, including the major problem of author rights. If a system like this were to be broadened into the general community where authors indeed make their livelihood from the royalties, revenues they receive from publishings, then there would be complications and certainly the authors would have to play at least a 50 percent role in any such determinations. I am certain that also they'll have to play some kind of a role in this proposed framework. At any rate, I'm here for the next day and I'll be glad to answer any questions.

PAUL ZURKOWSKI

SECONDARY INFORMATION SOURCES VIEW THE NEW COPYRIGHT ACT

Briefly what I'm going to tell you is a little bit about the information industry and provide a few glimpses at some of the problems that are remaining after the passage of the copyright revision act. The significance really of copyright is that it is an author-oriented piece of legislation. I'll try to separate out some evolving functions in the marketplace of information: the manufacturing function, the distribution function, and the retail function. And I hope this will suggest to you that some of the problems we're concerned with are derived not so much from copyright but from other evolutions in the relationships between the parties represented here. Finally, I'd like to suggest that I like the copyright office as an active participant on behalf of the constitutional provisions protecting the author's rights. There needs to be developed, because I don't think there is any on the scene today, a focal point for a national information policy which will help us separate out and make understandable some of the new relationships that are evolving as each of the organizations we work with develops and grows and is impacted by new technologies and new legislation. The program identifies my paper as dealing with the secondary information sources viewpoint. It would be easy enough to say that means ISI (Institute for Scientific

---

President, Information Industry Association.

108

Information) and its various *Current Contents* and University Microfilm in Ann Arbor, both of which function
something like a clearinghouse. They have copyright permission for many journal publications, and they offer
document fulfillment. If you aren't aware of them, you
might look into that aspect of solving the document fulfillment problem.

I'd like to take a very philosophic view of secondary
information publishing and test an idea or two with you.
Secondary information publishing is really a mixed-up
idea. So I would like to try to define it in terms of
information equivalent of events and artifacts. The information industry is involved in creating information
equivalents of every event and artifact that exists. Our
society entered the information age when more transactions occurred in information equivalence than occurred
in the actual events and artifacts themselves. And the
hallmark of the information business is the need, born
out of competition, to maintain the integrity of the relationships between event and artifact, and the particular information equivalent developed by a given company.
I think that's some of what Mr. Koch is talking about in
terms of an abstract. An abstract is, after all, an information equivalent for a way of getting at the primary
publication. He is concerned about maintaining the integrity of that abstract. This would be the report of
the scientific literature the abstract represents. I
suggest that ours is a very pluralistic society, not in
economic terms, but in terms of how we come at problems.
There may necessarily have to be a different abstract
written for a particular audience, one which is not an
informative abstract. This kind of abstract does not violate the copyright of the basic work and is itself perhaps an accepted copyrightable work. But abstracts are
information equivalents of journal articles and journal
articles are information equivalents to basic research,
right? Wrong. The real information equivalent of the
research that is conducted by a government or other research laboratory is contained in the notebook of the
laboratory technician who ran the protocols. That notebook details exactly what happened. I suggest for the
future that we will begin capturing such information
which is part of the neopublishing, so that in scien-

tific research you will be able to track trends in research by comparing the trends in research to the trends
in the basic laboratory experiments. Then we will be
able to do in science what the financial community is
doing in econometric models, if we can capture the information equivalent.

That's a new idea I've just thrown out to you. This
process is going on in other areas. There is a company
in Kensington, Maryland, that monitors television violence. It started out monitoring advertising on television because television stations blow so many commercials, and people spend a lot of money on commercials.
One station in Texas, incidentally, had been scratching
the Ford motor ads on Monday Night Football, running a
local Chevrolet ad in its place. The station was getting
paid from both ends. There is a need to monitor that
sort of thing, and so the monitoring company had people
watching television. That company worked out a definition of violence and came up with a way of correlating
the number of violent incidents on prime time television
with the advertisers who are supporting the programs. I
can give you the top ten most violent advertisers as
well as the top ten most violent programs. The monitoring company isn't dealing in anything published as such.
It's dealing in an information equivalent in an event
that occurred and was recorded off television.

A Massachusetts firm, International Data Corporation,
monitors the location of every computer facility in the
country. It creates a file of information equivalents -
the main frame, the peripherals, the kinds of people who
work there, the programmers, the systems analysts. This
is a great marketing tool for people who want to sell
equipment to those computer facilities. IDC markets that
file for about $12,000 a year. Occasionally it is ripped
off, as, for instance, when somebody gets a file, rekey-
boards it, and sells it as a $35 book. The company has
pursued such an incident, has gotten the sheriff to ar-
rest someone, and obtained court decisions requiring
that person not only to stop his rekeyboarding but to
pay IDC the proceeds of all the sales he made of the $35
book. That came about as a function of a state's unfair
competition law. It didn't have anything to do with copyright. This brings to mind a famous case involving a sex

book that originated at Indiana University in which
there was a question of unfair competition and infringement of copyright. It turned out that the remedy the
publisher had was not in copyright but unfair competition.

There are other data bases, as there are other financial fields. How does the research community market any
of that material? Right now it is marketed mostly under
the laws concerned with trade secrets and under unfair
competition regulations. Some of these data bases carry
a copyright notice. Some do not. There is no national
depository for that kind of material anywhere, because
the copyright law cannot do very much for material resulting from the new technologies. For that reason I
drew up a list of things I could have talked to you
about, and I'll just touch on some of these.

The Congress thought when it passed the copyright revision bill and enacted the bill creating the National
Commission on New Technological Uses of Copyrighted
Works that it had pretty well dealt with the new technologies. Unfortunately that was not so. There are some
things, largely problems of unfair competition, that are
going to fall between the cracks. Incidentally, there is
no federal statute that deals with unfair competition.
Problems of unfair competition rely on state laws for
remedy, and these vary from state to state. In the copyright revision bill Section 301, the federal preemption
statute, muddied that water some more with a floor amendment as to exactly how much of existing state unfair
competition law the federal copyright law preempts.

I could have talked about the position an in-print
publisher will be in when all he has is the right of
first publication. The author gives him neither the
right to photocopy nor any of the other rights that
Irwin Karp so accurately described. He will be in the
position essentially of the micropublisher of government
documents, in that he will not have control over the basic intellectual content of the material. That will be-
long to the author. What rights will a publisher be able
to pass on to a copy center? Will you as a librarian be
able to photocopy that work? Or will you be standing on
the shoulders of the publisher who did all of the work
of getting that material into the publication process?

Will you be, in the words of the INS case, reaping where you haven't sown? There are some nice questions of unfair competition mixed up in all of this. I've mentioned the absence of a national collection. I think it will be possible, should there ever be an unfair competition statute, to begin a national collection of some of those data bases if they were to be deposited under the philosophy of protection against unfair competition and were not then used by the depository in competition with the producer.

There is also the problem of compilation copyright that compounds the difficulties mentioned thus far. If you do make a compilation of any information equivalents you're entitled to a copyright for the entire compilation. The compilation copyright concept easily covers the situation in which one has selected 35 poems for a compilation of poetry, but is it really adequate for the publisher who has microrepublished the papers of the Confederacy, which consist of millions of documents? What are the choices of the publisher? Is a publisher able to copyright that material? If he copyrights it as a compilation can the Center for Research Libraries in Chicago advertise to its 180 members that it now has that collection and can photocopy ten or twenty of those without really destroying the market and without withdrawing all that stuff from the market? Is that fair competition? Would that be tolerated under the rules of unfair competition?

Similarly I could have talked about Section 602 of the Act which addresses the question of the importation of piratical copies, and I specifically make reference to the British Library Lending Division. What is the status of the NLM? NLM has become British Library Lending Division's major customer. What is the status of all those copies that NLM is getting out of there? And does the language of the Act really bestow responsibility for copyright enforcement of first class mail on the Customs Office?

I could have talked about the near disaster of the NTIS request for copyright protection in all NTIS documents. Where is the Office of Management and Budget? Where was the Copyright Office? That issue was discussed in 1958 and through 1961 and 1962; then it went away, but suddenly it reappeared. It turned up once more in the language of the House bill, from which it was almost impossible to dislodge, but implementation really would have created a lot of mischief.

The foregoing are some of the things I could have talked about. Now let me tell you what I think really you ought to know. I think that we need a national reevaluation of our priorities on information processes. I think we're at a watershed kind of situation. NSF has its task force taking a look at science information activities, reevaluating whether the Sputnik-age policy of funding . . . well, what the policy should be for the future. One of the people that made a presentation at a recent meeting of the task force, not its most recent meeting, was Vince Giuliano. He spelled out three eras that the information community in this country has gone through. One was predominant through World War II which he called the "information for information's sake" era. At that time, information was being market-pushed; that is, the information was being pushed out rather than the user trying to pull it out of the system. The second era was mission oriented: Atoms for Peace, Man on the Moon, that sort of thing, again heavily funded, heavily subsidized. We are now, according to Mr. Giuliano, in the problem-solving era, in which we have crossed disciplinary responsibility, an era in which the private sector has begun to provide some of the services that libraries and the government had provided in earlier eras. A market-pull rather than a market-push economics is operating now. There are literally hundreds of thousands, if not millions, of people involved in the process at this stage.

One of the things that I want to add to the foregoing scenario is a description of the market structure that is evolving. I contend that there is the manufacturing of data bases - the creative function, the distribution function, and the retail function. This market structure is based on the creation and marketing and distribution and use of information equivalents, so that if you want to buy the National Library of Medicine MEDLARS tapes, a manufactured product of NLM, to use in your own computers, the price is $50,000 a year, plus the cost of storing the information in your computer, and the cost

of using it. If you go to SDC, Lockheed, or BRS you can
probably gain access to the content of those files with
approximately a $5,000 investment in training, in leas-
ing of the equipment, and in computer time required to
train. You can, however, go to a retail outlet - and I
know you don't like the term "retail outlet," but it is
a transaction kind of activity, which doesn't necessarily mean that there is a money transaction at the time -
where, according to an NSF study made in 1975, there
were something like 146 machine-readable data bases con-
taining 46 million references to individual documents.
You can get that access through a retail information-on-
demand reference librarian at a cost perhaps of $50. As
you can see, it costs about $50,000 minimum to get into
the business, $5,000 if you deal with the distributor,
and about $50 at the on-demand or retail level. This
kind of service then is a cross-disciplinary problem-
solving service bringing those information equivalents
to bear on your particular problem. It is that very
process that is falling between the cracks at the National Commission, I mean the responsibility of the
Commission on New Technological Uses in the revision
bill. There are many problems in how that apparatus can
be made to be economically sound and viable. I think
that I will stop there and not try to deliver the next
45 minutes I've written out here.

DISCUSSION

Nancy Marshall (University of Wisconsin, Madison): I
  don't have any questions for anyone, but I have a
  general comment, which I must get out or I'll never
  be able to sleep tonight. What I've heard today is
  that some publishers at least are going to require
  the author to turn over their copyright as a condition of publishing the author's scholarly articles.
  I've also heard that authors of scholarly articles
  generated from research grant money most often pay
  to have their articles published. I've heard that no
  royalty payment will be paid to authors under the AAP
  Collection Center Concept, the AIP Concept, or what-

ever other concept may be developed. What bewilders
me is that during the long and arduous debate over
the past several years on the issue of library photocopying we all heard that it was the author whom the
publisher was protecting from the librarian. And I
respectfully submit that as with the great American
pastime, you can't always tell the players without a
score card.

Robert Frase: I'd like to make a very quick response to
that. The plan that presently is being pushed by the
AAP and will eventually be separated accommodates to
the possibility of publishers that want to be able to
pay their authors. It is possible by means of their
plan to have money go from the payment center to the
publisher and then to the author, depending upon the
specific arrangement that is involved there.

Bella Linden: I thought that it was rather clear that
there are many publishers and hundreds of thousands
of authors in this country who were not consulted by
the AAP, the trade association which promulgated this
plan. Those authors and those publishers who were not
consulted have not agreed to that plan. As a matter
of fact many of them have disassociated themselves
from that plan. I thought I had indicated clearly
that to my clients, and hundreds of thousands of authors believe that there is a partnership between the
authors and packagers of intellectual information, a
clearinghouse or a payment center requires that partnership to agree to the method of managing the photocopying clearinghouse or payment center, and that
certainly includes the payment of appropriate fees to
the partners I have identified. I've also identified
the librarians as those that ought to be, and many
are, in the forefront of protecting the author's and
publisher's rights, for their advantage and for the
advantage of this country as a whole. So I believe
that rather succinct statement may be a proper description of some, but certainly not of the majority,
and assuredly not of all.

Dale Middleton (University of Washington, Seattle): I expected Mr. Zurkowski to have some comments as well on

clearinghouse and payment schemes, but I would like
to ask all of the people who've spoken this afternoon
what their views of a reasonable royalty are. Mrs.
Linden said that the NTIS scheme would be too low in
its royalty offer, and Mr. Karp has expressed quite
strongly that there should be something added for authors in a royalty scheme. I wonder what a reasonable
royalty for publishers added to a reasonable royalty
to authors would amount to.

Irwin Karp: Well, you do not start bargaining royalties
in a conference like this and then have the other fel
low who's going to sit at the table and later say,
"Well, that's the starting point and we'll work our
way down from there." You would object if people sat
up here without being able to lay out all the factors
whether its a $600 a year/300 circulation translation
journal, or a $5.00 a year/100,000 circulation jour-
nal where the royalty may be just a few cents. There
are factors that have to be considered and this is
what we have been trying to set down and talk about
for five years with the American Library Association,
Association of Research Libraries, and the Special
Libraries Association. To date on the discussion of
precise figures, which we should have been in a position to give everybody including ourselves five years
ago, the problem is that we have not yet established
an agreement on the principle of whether there should
be payment. And there still has not been an agreement
on that. And in that context, as you would know, if
represented by a union, your union members wouldn't
even go in and start mentioning figures. I'm not about
to do it right now.

Paul Zurkowski: I would only note that the plan contem-
plates the publishers setting their own prices. And
that gets us very close to antitrust difficulties in
terms of agreeing on some price. I would only also
add that it's going to take some time to figure this
process out. It's going to be a process of trial and
error, and some publishers may price themselves out
of this market and continue to be photocopied outside
of the system at the risk of enforcement, at the risk
of being sued. There are details that you'll see in

the plan that Ben Weil has with him that have been
worked out by voluntary committees for maybe six
months with any degree of intensivity. On some of
these problems, the original Information Industry
Association position was that there should be a
three-year prototype experience to test out various
details in various areas until we figure out how it
works. Let me just give you one example. There is a
$260 a year translation journal that publishes 100
articles a year. If it becomes common knowledge that
you can buy or make a copy of a particular article
for $7.50, and you use the journal on the average of
10 times a year, what happens to the $260 subscrip-
tion? And if there are 120 subscribers at $260 per
subscription, how many of those 120 subscribers are
going to make the decision to discontinue the subscription because they can buy it for $7.50 a copy,
which to you sounds exorbitant, but which is a sum
that may doom that journal? It is a gamble for that
publisher. There isn't anything certain about it.

Ben Weil: Indiana University is conducting a study under
NSF sponsorship, in which it has circularized the
publishers for viewpoints and possible prices. I believe that when this study is published we will have
some information which will indicate what the publishers are thinking. It is not possible for the publishers to discuss these issues among themselves, but
it is possible for them to reply to the study, and I
think that we have to look for the first information
on this to come from that effort.

Herbert S. White: This is the study we are doing for
CONTU which Bob Frase mentioned and which is going
to be reported to him from the Research Center sometime in June.

Hardy Carroll (Western Michigan University): My question
is for Dr. Koch and it's about abstracts, specifically author abstracts. I think as a librarian and
information worker I know that I identify with the
physicists who want to get increased dissemination of
their works. Has AIP or any journal publisher that
you know of considered keeping copyright in the pri-

mary document, in the journal article, but having
the author go into the public domain so that the abstracts could be photocopied at will in order to en-
tice people to get the journal article, and hopefully
lead to more dissemination of the physicists' writing?

William Koch: You asked the simple question have we considered it; yes we have. The thing that is much more
of concern to us is not the photocopying of individual abstracts. Indeed we're not even too much concerned about the photocopying of every abstract from a
particular set of journals. The thing that does concern us is the use of computer-derived abstracts that
we could supply by means of the licensing of the tape
of abstracts that we produce. We can produce them
months before any other service can provide them. We
can provide them quite inexpensively, and what we
find is that there's going to be a competition of
these individually produced abstract services taking
our same abstracts and marketing them against the
product that we have available.

Hardy Carroll: Well, why couldn't you state after your
author abstracts that these are in the public domain
and they may be reproduced? That way you'd be leading
the way for all other journal publishers. Maybe they
could do the same thing.

William Koch: As I said, we are considering that, and
what we have to do is understand the complete implications of taking a position like that. It is awful-
ly simple to state it as you've stated it, but to
realize the detailed implications in the case of
large systematic reproducers is the thing that concerns us.

Hardy Carroll: Yes, there probably would have to be some
statement with regard to the general copyright statement in the introduction of the journal issue.

William Koch: We have developed a position of this sort
informally, but we're not in the position to describe
it publicly.

INTELLECTUAL PROPERTY AND INTELLECTUAL FREEDOM

ROBERT O'NEIL

My topic concerns a paradox that has been with us since the adoption of the Bill of Rights in 1791. The first amendment states that Congress shall make no law abridging the freedom of speech or of the press. Yet the copyright clause of Article I, section 8 appears to invite laws which have precisely that effect. From the earliest statute, through the 1909 version, to the revision of 1976, Congress has imposed injunctive and even criminal sanctions against expression of a certain kind - the unconsented communication of another person's protected intellectual property. The paradox is inescapable and requires some explanation.

The wonder is that so little has been said or written on this topic. When Zechariah Chafee, our preeminent first amendment scholar, wrote his treatise in 1941, he noted on the next to last of nearly 600 pages that "space does not permit comment on other topics affecting liberty of discussion, such as the law of copyrights," a slight which is the more remarkable in view of Chafee's major interest in the law of intellectual property. Thirty years later appeared a second major treatise, Thomas Emerson's *The System of Freedom of Expression*, this time without the barest reference to copyright law.

Vice-president, Indiana University - Bloomington, and Professor of Law.

In the year that Emerson's text appeared, however, two legal scholars almost simultaneously "discovered" the free speech-copyright conflict. Professor Paul Goldstein (then at Buffalo, now of Stanford) wrote a major article in the *Columbia Law Review*, warning of the need to reconcile conflicting values. Professor Melville Nimmer of UCLA wrote a shorter but equally concerned piece for his school's law review. The issue was at least out of the closet and before the legal community.

Meanwhile, several copyright defendants who had exhausted other avenues of extenuation pleaded that an infringement was justified by the first amendment. The courts rejected these claims, finding them - quite properly in most instances - to be thinly veiled attempts to raise the "fair use" defense through a different door. Now that the new law has been enacted and is soon to take effect, it is time to reexamine the paradox. What I should like to do is to look briefly at the nature of the confrontation, then to see how it has been accommodated under the 1909 act, and finally to carry the analysis into the new world of the copyright revision.

Let us look first at the current relationship between protection for free expression and for intellectual property. Surely the two bodies of law are not entirely concurrent. Various forms of expression enjoy first amendment protection but cannot claim copyright protection. The publication, for example, of public domain works, or of excerpts from government publications, clearly come within freedom of speech or of the press. Even statements which lack the degree of originality required for copyright protection - graphs, schedules, charts, and the like - presumably come within the purview of the first amendment (though as a practical matter one who publishes such material is unlikely to care much about constitutional protection).

A similar divergence runs in the opposite direction. Many forms of expression that lie beyond the borders of the first amendment are nonetheless copyrightable. Perhaps the most obvious category is practical objects, like the chimpanzee lamp bases in *Mazer* vs. *Stein*, or the lighting fixture held in a very recent case to be a "writing" - even though they would hardly constitute "speech" for first amendment purposes. Advocacy which

might be criminally punishable as incitement, or "fighting words" which fall outside the first amendment, are
also proper subjects for copyright. Fraudulent and de-
ceptive publications may send the author or publisher to
jail, but - as a federal court of appeals has recently
held - he takes with him a claim for infringement against
anyone who copies without permission. Commercial advertising, which until very recently was not protected by
the first amendment, has always enjoyed copyright protection. Most obscene material is probably protected by
the copyright law, though a federal judge in Texas last
fall drew the line for copyright purposes at the point
where material becomes punishable as pornography. In
short, there is some concurrence but far from complete
symmetry between the two categories of federally protected expression.

Even if the *scope* of protection is not identical, the
purposes may be consonant. Professor Goldstein makes the
point forcefully: "The Government's grant of the copyright monopoly tends to abridge the community's right to
hear. Yet, from a broader perspective, copyright may be
perceived as serving to advance this right. . . . Copyright, by providing the economic incentive to the production of artistic expression, theoretically ensures
that the range of subject matter disseminated will include that which is promoted by profit considerations
and will not be left merely to the chance of political
motivation."

Despite such reassurances, the conflict remains.
Copyright remedies inhibit the free publication and distribution of materials which would otherwise be protected speech or press. It is thus appropriate to ask
how we manage to live with this dilemma. A first answer
has superficial appeal, but only that. Both provisions,
after all, are in the Constitution. But, as Professor
Nimmer has pointed out, "the first amendment is an
amendment, hence superseding anything inconsistent with
it that may be found in the main body of the Constitution." If, therefore, Congress really meant "no law" in
the first amendment, as Mr. Justice Black suggested in
his later years, then we might have to strike the copyright clause by implication. It would be rather late in
the day to read the terms so literally; even Justice

Black, much less the other Justices, most attuned to
first amendment claims, never so argued.

Instead, we must somehow find an accommodation between the two systems of protection, and hope that the
cases as well as the new statute reasonably well fit
that accommodation. What I shall suggest is that a tac-
it accommodation does exist and that it is reasonably
satisfactory to both sets of interests. Let me outline
briefly the elements in the present law which provide
the accommodation.

One such element is the absence of copyright protection for government publications - Section 8 of the current law. This provision ensures that copyright will not
be used as a form of censorship, as it was during the
early history of British copyright, and as it still is
even today in some totalitarian nations. Professor (now
Justice) Benjamin Kaplan remarked of the monopoly exercised by the British Stationer's office in the 16th and
17th centuries, "copyright had the look of being gradually secreted in the interstices of censorship." Since
the elimination of a substantive role for the Stationer's
office and the Statute of Anne in 1710, all that is ancient history, at least as far as the Western copyright
system is concerned.

Second, I would point to the limited term of protection for published (and registered unpublished) works.
The constitutional clause does speak of "limited terms"
and the statutes have always reflected that constraint.
Moreover, when material passes into the public domain,
neither federal nor state law can extend the period of
protection. Equally important, otherwise protectible
material published in a manner that fails to meet the
statutory requirements - even in a most technical way,
such as claiming a later than actual publication date -
forfeits protection and is forever irretrievable. Thus
the terms and conditions of protection are limited
in important ways, at least for published works.

Third, the copyright law draws a vital distinction
between the *idea* (which is not protected) and the *expression* (which may be protected). In the one reference
to this issue in the Supreme Court reports, Justice
Douglas cautioned: "Serious first amendment questions
would be raised if Congress's power over copyrights

were construed to include the power to grant monopolies over ideas. . . . The arena of public debate would be quiet, indeed, if a politician could copyright his speeches or a philosopher his treatise and thus obtain a monopoly on the ideas they contain. We should not construe the copyright laws to conflict so patently with the values that the First Amendment was designed to protect."

The idea/expression distinction harks back to our opening discussion. Freedom of speech and of the press protects the idea more than the expression, while the reverse is true of copyright. The distinction is clearly reflected in the 1959 Supreme Court decision which spared the film version of *Lady Chatterly's Lover* from a finding of obscenity because it *advocated* - rather than merely *depicting* - adultery. A unanimous Court observed that "the First Amendment's basic guarantee is of freedom to advocate ideas." This stress upon protection for the idea furthers the accommodation between copyright and free speech.

A fourth, and hitherto unnoticed factor, I believe, is the absence from American copyright law of the doctrine of moral right. Most European countries recognize in the author or creator an interest in personality or reputation which goes beyond the rights enumerated in our law. Thus an author may object to the manner in which a painting is displayed, or a book edited, or a play revised for movies or television. We have resisted such notions in our law, save to the extent they may be recognized by principles of contract, tort, or unfair competition. Recently, there has been much discussion about the Monty Python case, in which a federal court of appeals enjoined the alleged mutilation by an American network of certain episodes of the BBC comic series. But the rationale for the decision was not moral right in the European sense, even though the result and some of the language might so imply. (Let me offer a caution here: I do not oppose limited recognition of moral right; in fact I feel our courts may have been too abstemious in this area. But any reception of the European doctrine into the American law which would, for example, restrict parodies and satires to any greater degree than they are now restricted, would raise serious first amendment issues and should be approached with caution.)

A fifth and quite familiar element of accommodation is the doctrine of fair use. American law permits the unconsented copying of limited portions of a copyrighted work for certain purposes. The scope of this privilege will depend on the nature of the material, the amounts copied, and the effects of the copying on the proprietor's interests. There is also an important value transcending the immediate parties, "whether a distribution would serve the public interest in the free dissemination of information and whether its preparation requires some use of prior materials dealing with the same subject matter." Although it is not crucial whether the copying is done for profit, the fair use claims of educational, scientific and literary copiers have tended to fare better than those of others.

Related to the fair use doctrine is one other principle of American copyright law which should perhaps have been mentioned earlier. Obvious though it may seem, it is important that our law does not permit any person to copyright facts, news or events. The Supreme Court observed more than a half century ago in the *International News Service* case: "It is not to be supposed that the framers of the Constitution . . . intended to confer upon one who might happen to be the first to report a historic event the exclusive right for any period to spread the knowledge of it." (It is true that the majority in the *INS* case, over Justice Brandeis' vigorous dissent did end up enjoining the use of wire service stories by a competitor, though on unfair competition misappropriation rather than copyright grounds.)

This overview of the present accommodation brings us to a final issue under the present law. Is there or should there be a first amendment defense not covered by any of the foregoing principles? For the most part courts have viewed first amendment claims as back door attempts to reopen rejected or frivolous fair use claims. Yet Professor Nimmer wisely warns that a grave danger to copyright may lie in the failure to distinguish between the statutory privilege known as fair use and an emerging constitutional limitation on copyright contained in the first amendment. Nimmer goes on to

argue that in certain situations - the Zapruder film of
the John Kennedy assassination being his prime example -
a first amendment interest should be recognized even
though fair use might not permit copying. Professor
Goldstein has advanced two "accommodative principles,"
the first of which is most germane here: "that copyright
infringement be excused if the subject matter of the infringed material is relevant to the public interest and
the appropriator's use of the material independently advances the public interest."

There is neither time nor occasion here to apply the
Nimmer or Goldstein tests to actual cases. The plain
fact is that a legitimate first amendment claim is seldom raised. When it does arise, it is often coextensive
with a valid fair use claim - as in the case of the
Julius and Ethel Rosenberg letters, finally resolved
last July by a summary judgment on fair use grounds in
favor of the defendants. For me the most troubling case
is that of the ghetto priests in St. Louis who several
years ago performed "Jesus Christ Superstar" without
permission of the authors, while the musical was still
much in demand. Since their performance was partly an
act of protest, they raised a first amendment claim
quite distinct from any privilege of fair use. The court
was troubled, but finally held the priests to be pirates
with respect to the work in question; protest or other
good motives alone would not excuse an otherwise blatant infringement. I suspect Professors Goldstein and
Nimmer would agree with the decision, though it post-
dates their articles.

As for the other cases in which the first amendment
issue has been discussed - notably the use of Walt
Disney's Mickey Mouse cartoon characters by a group
calling themselves (prophetically) "the Air Pirates" -
I do not perceive a free speech claim that transcends
the fair use defense. As the court observed in the
Disney case: "To extend the First Amendment protection
to cover this case would serve to obliterate copyright
protection in any instance in which the alleged in-
fringer could claim the intent to convey an idea."

My conclusion, then, is that the actual accommodation
under the current law is at least tolerable, even if not
always conscious. But we now have a new dimension, since

the 1909 law will soon give way to its much more detailed successor. It is therefore essential to update
this analysis by carrying our speculation beyond next
January. In looking ahead, I find the accommodation under the new law better in two quite distinct ways: one,
because of some actual substantive changes which favor
the interest in free expression, and two, because of
rather precise codification of previously uncertain common law accommodative principles. I will touch briefly
on four provisions by way of illustration.

First, there is the elimination of common law protection for unpublished works through the uniform federal
system of Section 301. This provision favors free expression partly by limiting the term of protection for
all works, whether published or unpublished. It also ensures uniformity of substantive law in the future by
preempting all state protection for interests akin to
those of copyright. Thus persons who wish to use protected material will know when it has passed into the
public domain, and by what legal principles the extent
of protection will be judged.

Second, the definition of protected works is helpful.
Section 102 excludes from copyright protection ideas,
procedures, processes and the like, thus drawing clearly
in the statute a line which until now has been left to
the vagaries of judicial determination. Of course, some
ambiguity remains in the terms, and decisions will be
required under the new law as under the old, but at
least the broad contours of protection will be more
clearly marked.

Third, the accommodation will benefit from the statutory recognition of fair use in Sections 107 and 108.
Such provisions do exist in the laws of most other Western countries, and it is high time we had such safeguards here. Although Section 107 largely codifies the
previous understanding of fair use, that is helpful in
and of itself. And as I hardly need to remind this audience of experts, Section 108 resolves some previously
troublesome ambiguities, even if it does not go as far
in the direction of free expression as many librarians
and teachers would have wished.

A fourth and final provision that may be helpful is
Section 113 c. This clause permits the use of photo-

graphs in commentaries and news reports of useful articles which incorporate protected pictorial works. While
such a right of criticism or comment was implied under
the prior law, the explicit recognition of "news reports"
as a valid medium for this purpose aids the accommodation.

While the new law does represent a substantial improvement, there may be one or two cautions. The interests of free expression are not well served by the extension in Section 304 of subsisting copyright terms although the reasons for that extension are as well understood as the last minute change in the West German copyright revision from a term of life plus fifty years to
life plus seventy at the behest of the heirs of Richard
Strauss.

A more serious and substantive problem may arise from
the very clarity with which certain matters previously
left to the courts have now been spelled out by the Congress. There is an ancient maxim in the law: inclusio
unius, exclusio alterius est. The maxim means that the
codification of one principle, or exception, implies
that others which are similar and might have been included were deliberately left out. Take, for example,
the enumeration in Section 107 of the factors by which
the defense of fair use is to be judged. Two implications arise: one, that other factors which might have
entered under the common law should not now be enter-
tained; and two, that a fair use-like defense which does
not meet these criteria should no longer be allowed.
Thus the further development of the embryonic first
amendment defense may be inhibited by the very specificity of Sections 107 and 108.

On the other hand, Professor Nimmer is certainly
right that Congress cannot restrict by statute the recognition of a constitutional defense. The tension between intellectual property and intellectual freedom,
in short, inheres in our very constitutional structure.
It has been with us for a long time, and doubtless will
survive the revision of the copyright law. All we can
hope to do is to understand this paradox a bit better
and deal with it in the rare case which genuinely presents it.

DISCUSSION

Unidentified: Mr. O'Neil, did you hear what I heard the
other day in the news about Carter's advisers looking
into copyright as a way of protecting documents from
future Pentagon Papers situations? Or can that be
just rejected out of hand as a bright idea from the
wrong track?

Robert O'Neil: I'm not even sure I would reject it as a
bright idea. The question, in case you didn't hear
it, was a suggestion of which I was not aware, by
some people in the Carter Administration, that future
Pentagon Paper affairs might be prevented by some
kind of protection for executive memoranda and the
like. Unless these were treated completely as private
documents, I see no way in which such a theory would
survive the very clear injunction against copyright
protection for government publications. The line is
most clearly suggested by two cases with which some
of you may be familiar. One case involved Admiral
Rickover's speeches. The claim was made that Admiral
Rickover's speeches were not a proper subject for
copyright because he had used some government papers,
and some of them had been typed by his secretary at
the Pentagon. The Court of Appeals, I think properly,
though not without some difficulty, concluded that
these were not what the present law means in Section
8 as government publications, even though there was
some limited governmental involvement. It is of
course true that Congress can define, for purposes
of withholding or exclusion from copyright protection,
what is meant by government publications, and occasionally a specific statute will contain a provision
that a certain kind of federally funded program may
or may not take copyright in the resulting publications.
   The other case involves a group of soldiers who on
their spare time at a military base, I think it was
Fort Dix, made a statue. The purpose of the statue
was, I think, to grace the entrance. It was something
like the mounting of the flag at Iwo Jima, some noble
event in military history. Inexplicably, a match com-

pany came along and copied in two dimensional form
this three dimensional statue and put it on the covers of their match books. One of the soldiers, having
been released from the service and now a private cit-
izen, sued the match company. The match company
claimed that since the statue had been produced on
government time, on Army time, so to speak, it was
therefore a government document and soldiers could
not sue the match company as private citizens for
having misappropriated their work of art. The artistic value was conceded to be somewhat limited, but I
spoke earlier about the outdoor lighting fixture
which goes far beyond the chimpanzees on the lamp
base in terms of utilitarian works defined as being a
"writing." Well, I must confess I've forgotten the
outcome of the case of the statue. My recollection is
that the court did not accept the match company's argument that the statue was a government document under Section 8. Those, to me, are the two cases that
really test the issue. Now, in order to provide anything like copyright protection for executive memo-
randums, it would certainly be necessary for Congress
to do what had occasionally been done, by special
provision, to say, "These things are not government
documents as defined in the statute." That's perfectly proper. It is only a statutory dispensation, although, as I suggested earlier the history of the
Stationers Company makes me think that there's at
least a little constitutional underpinning in the
withholding of protection for government documents.
I at least feel much more comfortable if that's a
firm part of our law.

Question Not Recorded:

Robert O'Neil: That seems to me to be a clear example of
   something which doesn't raise the first amendment issue beyond whatever defense derives from Section 107.
   I am assuming, by the way, that there is no Section
   111 issue. (The question is whether taping off the air
   of TV programs for classroom use may be protected by
   fair use, or if not, to some extent by the first
   amendment argument.) I don't think that there is any
   special nonuse type interest that would properly come

within the first amendment claim in this case. I suspect one first has to look carefully, because the new
statute is so detailed in this regard, at all the
things provided in Sections 110 and 111 with respect
to TV broadcasting. If you conclude that this kind of
taping would not be enjoinable under the specific
broadcasting provisions, that is a good example of
the "inclusio unius, exclusio alterius est" argument;
that is, the implication that Congress said everything they could conceivably say about appropriation
of broadcast in this enormously complex structure
they've set up in Sections 110 and 111, and if they
didn't cover this situation, then they probably meant
to exempt it. With that background it seems to me a
quite plausible fair use argument could be made at
least for taking a single copy for a noncommercial
use in a classroom for education purposes.

Question Not Recorded:

Robert O'Neil: The question is, if it were a documentary,
not a dramatic work, does the free speech argument
have any more mileage? Again I think not, because the
fair use doctrine recognizes this factor; that is,
the extent to which a line moves across a continuum
from works created by the proprietors - the literary
end of the scale - over to events observed by the proprietor, an extreme example being, of course, the
Zapruder film of the Kennedy assassination in Dallas.
The reason that I'm troubled by Nimmer's use of the
Zapruder home movie case as a first amendment case is
because I've always thought fair use went very far in
that direction anyway. It seems to me that a proper
fair use argument would encompass most of that continuum. Now he argues that the Zapruder film is different
because, there being only one person there with a
movie camera, you cannot describe meaningfully the
assassination of John F. Kennedy without access to
the Zapruder film. Thus the film becomes the only
tangible embodiment of the event. And for that reason he argues that there should be a First Amendment
access transcending normal fair use access. I agree
that's an unusual case.

Unidentified: You said that we could make a single copy for classroom use. What about the librarian?

Robert O'Neil: I didn't say anyone could make a single copy of anything. Let me repeat, I said if that situation is not covered by Sections 110 and 111, then I believe one could make a respectable, substantial 107 argument. I don't want to go further than that. I am licensed as an attorney in the Commonwealth of Massachusetts. I have no license to practice in Indiana, and therefore my purporting to give any advice as definitive as that would constitute the unauthorized practice of law, and I've got to be careful about that. I will therefore go no further than to say I believe that this situation presents a persuasive claim of fair use, but I don't want to say any more than that. The library question becomes a little more complex because, as I understand 107, the single immediate classroom educational use may be a little more clearly protected than recording for permanent storage purposes, with the possibility that subsequent uses from the collection in which the tape is placed will not be as clearly within the purview of Section 107's purposes as the teacher's original morning-after presentation for the class. Therefore, I think one is probably getting on a little shakier ground as one moves into a more permanent kind of storage, but I want to be as clear as I can that I'm not purporting to give answers, not only because I'm not a member of the Indiana bar, but also because this is not presently my field.

Session 2

April 15, 1977

ROBERT WEDGEWORTH

HOW THE AMERICAN LIBRARY ASSOCIATION VIEWS THE NEW COPYRIGHT ACT

What I plan to do is to give you an overall perspective, both from the point of view of the American
Library Association, of which I am Executive Director,
and from the perspective of the National Commission on
New Technological Uses of Copyrighted Works (CONTU), an
agency responsible for advising the Congress with regard
to the new Copyright Act of 1976. I would also like to
review briefly some of the major events which brought us
up to the passage of the law, so that you will understand the positions that have been held for several
years.

The most significant statement that the library community made about the prospects of a revision of the
1909 Copyright Law came in testimony which we presented
before the House Committee on the Judiciary, Subcommittee on Courts, Civil Liberties, and the Administration
of Justice, chaired by Representative Kastenmaier of
Wisconsin. In that testimony we indicated that the library community had a number of major concerns about
the copyright bill, S 22.

First, we were concerned about the discriminatory
treatment being given to special libraries which are
subordinate units in for-profit corporations, but which

Executive Director, American Library Association, and
member, National Commission on New Technological Uses of
Copyrighted Works.

have contributed greatly to the research and educational
activities in this country by making their resources
available to specialists. We were concerned about the
proposed requirement that librarians, or rather library
employees, be aware that several users may have need of
copies of a particular journal article, whether they
express this need together or on separate occasions over
some unspecified period of time. We were concerned about
the prohibition of an undefined activity called "systematic reproduction" which becomes a "code" for library
photocopying practices thought to be injurious to copyright proprietor interests. We were concerned about the
limitations proposed for excluding musical works, pictorial works, graphic and other audiovisual works from
rights granted in the case of other materials. Our question was: "Are the needs of a music historian so very
much different from other scholars that they cannot be
routinely met with copies of their research materials?"
In addition to these concerns which were prominently expressed in this testimony, we had other general concerns
about the bill, and I will simply mention one which remains of concern to us. Why is it necessary for unpublished materials to have the same copyright terms as
published materials, when in the supporting documentation provided to the Congress it was made clear that
approximately 85 percent of these materials do not have
their copyrights renewed at the end of the first term?
The implication that we saw for making this change in
unpublished materials, predominantly manuscript materials held by many research libraries, was that there was
going to be a welter of confusion surrounding who owns
the rights to such materials when the terms under which
the materials are donated to libraries and archives,
are unspecified. Now we all know, and I'm sure that
you've heard on more than one occasion, including yesterday, that the implications of the constitutional basis for copyright imply that there is a significant public policy question.

   During the course of the debates, controversies, and
discussions in which I participated, various groups
tended to come down on one side or the other as the issues were raised. The public policy questions became
lost in a welter of accusations, publicity stunts, and

Congressional lobbying. But now we have a new copyright law. I think it's important for us to put all of these events behind us, look at our current situation, and determine what the future is likely to be. First, the law is extremely complex. It deals with such ambiguous factors as the concept of fair use which has achieved statutory status for the first time, special exemptions for various purposes, and the still vague concept of systematic reproduction and it is supplemented by informal guidelines accepted by the Congress but which are not embodied in the law dealing with classroom photocopying and photocopying for interlibrary loan purposes.

There are no simple answers to all of the questions that vexed the principals involved in the copyright law. The new law imposes record retention requirements on libraries that we have never had before. It requires a new level of awareness as to administrative practices regarding coin-operated photocopying machines, as well as machines that are under the direct supervision of libraries. It does not resolve the most troublesome issues primarily because we do not as yet fully understand the new technological environment in which publishers, librarians, and authors are all involved. What about off-the-air taping of broadcasts? What about the computer uses of copyrighted works, a topic which has been directly assigned to the National Commission on New Technological Uses of Copyrighted Works? Fair use has been given statutory recognition, but it still lacks a clearly defined public policy framework.

In spite of all of these problems, it is our opinion that the law is workable. We have bought time in terms of the most pressing issues that face all of the principals involved in copyright, but we must recognize that we have only temporized on the technological issues. What then does the law have of significance for librarians? In addressing the law, we need to begin with the concept of fair use. This statutory provision limits the amount of copying which can be done without permission from copyright proprietors or without payment. There are four major criteria for assessing fair use: (1) the purpose and character of the use, including whether it is a commercial or nonprofit purpose; (2) the nature of the copyrighted work itself; (3) the amount

and substantiality of the portion used in relation to
the work as a whole; and (4) the effect of that use on
the potential market for or value of the copyrighted
work.

These criteria are fraught with problems of measure-
ment and definition. How much is substantial? A very
tiny portion of a highly expensive physics journal is
much more significant than four articles from an issue
of a journal in another field. How do you measure the
potential market for or value of a copyrighted work?
From some data made available by the British Library
Lending Division, we know that the value of copyrighted
journals in the scientific area has declined signifi-
cantly over the past several years. This decline in
value is attributed to (1) the reduction in the size of
the journal; and (2) the increase in price in relation
to the size of the journal. Another factor is the decline in advertising which has resulted in an increase
of the subscription price. Put simply, an increase in
price for the same amount of material is a decline in
value. What is a nonprofit educational use as distinct
from a commercial use? This is a question which remains
very much unresolved for special libraries, and I expect that Mr. Gonzalez will address this question. Fair
use can cover multiple copying for classroom use as well
as the single copying which is normal for libraries.
There are special guidelines which have been developed
to address these major topics. The special guidelines
for classroom copying and for educational uses of music,
as well as for interlibrary loans, provide guidance on
what the major interested parties thought reasonable.
They do not appear in the statute but are included in
the conference report on the bill. These guidelines will
facilitate the implementation of the law but, in the
final analysis, will simply beg the question of public
policy with respect of the use of material under copyright.

Throughout the long, torturous history of the Williams
and Wilkins litigation, the American Library Association
maintained that library photocopying is absolutely essential to the effective dissemination and use of information for purposes of research and study. We recognized
that individual libraries can no longer consider them-

selves to be self-sufficient. We also recognized that
the national libraries have been enormously successful
in removing the geographical barriers to gaining access
to various research materials for students and scholars.
This has been done in many ways, ranging from the sophisticated resource-sharing networks such as MINITEX
in Minnesota to the very simple device of the Louisiana
Numerical Register. In the latter they simply list the
Library of Congress numbers of materials held in various
libraries in Louisiana, provide this list on microfilm,
and use it as the basis for interlibrary loans.

Although the American Library Association is still
studying the law and will make available more precise
advisory statements, the new law will allow virtually
everything that librarians wanted in the law under certain terms and conditions. The new law provides no simple answers to the most vexing problems which fueled the
controversy over copyright. However, the new law may require further agreements by the principals in order to
implement it effectively. Example: Libraries under Section 108 (the special exemptions provided to libraries
and archives) can continue to provide single copies in
lieu of interlibrary loans, up to six in a given year
from a given journal within five years of publication.
Libraries can, at the request of the instructor, provide
multiple copies which meet the test of brevity and spontaneity under the guidelines for educational uses for
classroom purposes. I think those are two significant
examples. We cannot at this point give more precise procedures as to how libraries should go about this. This
is one of the things that you should expect prior to
January 1, 1978. The new law, in our opinion, does not
answer questions regarding certain specific problems.
Who has rights to unpublished materials given to libraries under unspecified terms? What constitutes a reasonable effort to determine the availability of materials
under copyright which a library wishes to purchase?
What constitutes a fair price for materials under such
circumstances? It is useful for us to look at these
questions from the eyes of librarians and copyright
proprietors in other countries, who are also wrestling
with this phenomenon.

The Whitford Report which was presented to the Par-

liament of the United Kingdom just last month is a study
of reprography. In the summary of recommendations, you
will find it interesting to note their conclusions.
There should be a flexible system of blanket licensing
to cater to all use requirements for facsimile copies
including library, educational, government, industrial,
and professional copying, but there should be no compulsory license to publish. We see this concept as a most
dangerous precedent in terms of our ability to acquire
and disseminate information in the United States. The
implication of that recommendation is that the government of the United Kingdom must set up a blanket licensing procedure which inevitably requires a clearinghouse
for the payment of all royalties for all copies that are
made from copyrighted works, especially by libraries. It
also denies compulsory licensing which, in effect, means
that there is the ability to suppress materials, either
deliberately or by failing to reply to requests for permission to copy. We view this concept as a significant
danger to libraries in this country, not because we do
not need clearinghouses to provide rapid access to materials that libraries do not own, but because we do not
believe that these clearinghouses should become compulsory in terms of our use.

Let me just share with you a very penetrating comment
as to why a clearinghouse is necessary. I'm quoting from
an article published in *Serials Review* July-September
1976. "No publisher will expect to perform promptly the
research job needed for a permission, even if paid. Such
jobs are generally assigned when the current work load
is subsiding, which unfortunately means indefinite de-
lays." Now we know that the distribution of copyrighted
materials in this country is a highly centralized and
ineffective system. At the same time, we recognize that
the informal system of resource-sharing and interlibrary
loans among libraries and other information centers has
vastly supplemented this primary distribution system. We
must improve not only the primary system from the copyright proprietors, but enhance the interlibrary loan and
other resource-sharing systems that libraries have devel
oped. A second recommendation which the Whitford Committee made was that the copyright owners be encouraged to
set up such schemes.

If such clearinghouses become a fact - and, in my opinion, it is inevitable that there will be some - we should encourage them under several different auspices, primarily because there are two major differences in the type of publications that libraries are normally inclined to acquire. First, you have the commercial publishers and those authors who publish for profit. Secondly, you have the scientific society-type publication. We believe that it is not necessary to combine these two types of publishing in the same clearinghouse, since their objectives are entirely different. Most scientific societies are established in order to disseminate information to those members who are interested in that particular academic subject. The reward that the authors have for writing in such journals is the recognition of their peers, and this is the primary currency within scientific fields. On the other hand, much of the most important materials by many authors, some of whom write for a living, that we need to acquire is made available through commercial publishers. We must respect the rights of all authors and publishers, but at the same time examine the primary purposes for which they are making their materials available. I would like to contrast briefly the major recommendations that I have read to you from the Whitford Report from Great Britain, with the report of the Copyright Law Committee on Reprographic Reproduction of Australia.

Recommendation Number 1.45: "In the application of the fair dealing provisions," (fair dealing is their term for fair use, provisions for reprographic reproduction) "it is our unanimous view that the section" (of the Australian Copyright Law) "should be widened to allow such reproduction for the purpose of research or study, instead of research or private study." In addition, "two of us" (two members of the committee) "would extend those purposes to purposes such as research, study, private, or personal use." This recommendation would apply whether the copying is being done on a self-service machine or other machine, and whether the machine is in a library or elsewhere. *Recommendation Number 1.46*: "We also recommend that limited multiple-copying of single articles and any periodical for use in the libraries of nonprofit educational establishments be

allowed without remuneration to the copyright owners."
Recommendation Number 1.49: "We recommend that certain
requirements should exist with self-service machines in
libraries, namely that notices and a form prescribed by
regulation should be displayed, drawing attention to the
relevant provisions of the Copyright Act. If this is
done, the installation and use of self-service copying
machines in a library should not of itself impose any
liability upon the owner of the library for any copyright infringement committed by a user of a machine."
This is similar to the provision in the U.S. law. *Recommendation Number 1.52*: "We received sufficient evidence
on the extent of multiple copying in educational establishments for us to conclude that it is likely that some
of the copying thus taking place is an infringement of
copyright under the existing law. We also think that the
demand for such copying will increase. To the extent
that there is a demand, the copyright law should accommodate this demand. However, in principle, we consider
that multiple copying should not be carried out without
remuneration to the copyright owner in any case where it
represents a substantial use of his property, or it
could prejudice sales of his work, particularly if the
work has been specifically written for use in the
schools."

Those provisions indicate clearly that we are not
isolated in trying to struggle through the difficulties
in arriving at a new copyright law which is consistent
with the new technological capabilities available not
only to individuals but to schools, libraries, and other
educational institutions, as well as to libraries in the
private commercial sector. We must proceed toward further agreement between librarians and copyright proprietors, the publishers and authors. The characteristics of
these agreements will have to recognize the facts of
what is occurring in each of our lives every day. An
alarming prospect is that we may push toward development
which ignore all that we know about the operation of libraries and all that we know about the characteristics
and behavior of scholars. For example, we know that the
distribution of interests and activity for photocopying
purposes across the range of materials that are available for copyright is highly centralized. There are a

few journals and other types of materials which will
get high use and there are many other journals and other
types of materials which will get little or no use. We
would hope, as we move toward developing agreements under which limited copying will be available for educational and research purposes, that all such agreements
will recognize this. One of the clear implications of
establishing a major system to take care of the photocopying which may occur under isolated and unrelated
conditions is that there will be a few publishers and
authors who will do very well, and there will be many
other publishers and authors who will receive little or
no benefit from such developments. It is for this reason
that I would reemphasize that we must take a look at
whether there should not be some distinctions between
the types of arrangements that are made for various
types of publications.

The National Commission on New Technological Uses of
Copyrighted Works has as its primary role the analysis
of the activity and the provision of an environment in
which agreements between principals in the copyright
controversy can take place. A good example of this is
the agreement which resulted in the guidelines for photocopying activity related to interlibrary loans. We
have not solved this question, but we have brought the
principals into closer proximity. There is a great need
for more accurate data on which to base future agreements. There are clear prospects for this in the study
which has been sponsored by CONTU and the National Commission on Library and Information Science. This study,
commonly called the King Report, will provide for the
first time a clear and accurate look at the photocopying
activity which presently goes on in various types of libraries, probably the most significant piece of information on photocopying since the data provided by the
British Lending Library.

Certainly, there are no definite answers which can be
presented about photocopying activity and the prospects
of how this will relate to the implementation of the new
copyright law. The issues that were before us prior to
its passage still remain with us, though the principals
are less strident in their demands, and the agreements
that bind us force us to negotiate with each other. For

those of you in the library world who are concerned, I have one final word of assurance for you. In a recent article written by Michael Cardosa, an attorney, he suggests that probably the best protection librarians have is that none of us really understands the copyright law. And, in the absence of such understanding, we might suggest that it is one of the few examples where innocence can be a valid excuse.

DISCUSSION

Susan Brynteson (Indiana University): It is my observation that it is the first time on the national level that the six library associations worked together to implement legislation. The Medical Library Association, the Music Library Association, the American Association of Law Librarians, ARL, ALA, and SLA. I believe you have played a key leadership role in this respect. It seems to me that is a fine fringe benefit of the tortuous new copyright law, and I wonder if you would comment on this as a trend for the future regarding implementation or enactment of legislation at the national level.

Robert Wedgeworth: Well, I think it was a very significant development. One of the interesting aspects of it was that we all discovered that we liked each other. We recognize that we have too many interests in common to remain widely separated. The future of special libraries is inextricably related to the future of other types of libraries. The resources that they bring to bear on the educational and research environment in this country are tremendous. Therefore we had to coordinate our efforts to remain as a system. With the National Plan which has been developed by the National Commission, we see that it is inevitable that we are moving toward some kind of coordinated national library and information system. If that is so, we feel that it is a primary necessity for us to consult with each other and negotiate points of difference in order to arrive at mutually agreed-upon objectives.

Audrey Michaels (Allisonville, Indiana, Elementary School): My teachers are terribly concerned about just what they can copy. In your talk, you said that special guidelines have been written, but they did not appear in the bill. They were in the conference report on the bill, and I would like to know how I could get a copy of that for my teachers.

Robert Wedgeworth: I am glad you asked, because we originally published the guidelines in a special issue of the ALA *Washington Newsletter*, dated November 15, 1976. This is a summary of all of the issues in the new copyright law that we felt were of interest to librarians. The demand for that special issue was so high that we reprinted it as a separate. This reprint is available from the American Library Association in Chicago. It contains all of the guidelines and all of the major provisions that affect libraries.

Jean Leffers (Fort Wayne, Indiana, Public Library): I believe I read in that *Washington Newsletter* that the ALA was going to come out with a new form for interlibrary loans. Do you know if anything has been solved on that?

Robert Wedgeworth: Yes, as a matter of fact, the members of the committee who are working on the new interlibrary loan form are here at this conference and have had several meetings or rump sessions as you might call them, in addition to their formal proceedings. But it is not just the new interlibrary loan form. Let me just briefly list some of the things we will need to develop between now and the first of January. There needs to be a notice of copyright which is to be placed adjacent to all unsupervised copying machines in libraries, and the text of that notice will have to be approved by the Register of Copyright. The interlibrary loan form needs to be revised in order to conform to the record resolution requirements of the new law as it pertains to interlibrary arrangements, but we do not plan to stop there because we believe that the ALA should advise, in consultation

with our other sister associations, on a complete record retention policy for all libraries, since we
will need this data as time passes in order to assess
what happens out in the field. The Register of Copyright will need this data in order to perform adequately the five-year review that is required by the
new copyright law. In addition, there are a number of
other tasks which will have to be completed. We will
have to define what a "reasonable effort" to attain
access to materials may be through the search of
"commonly known trade sources." As a former acquisitions librarian, I know of no tool which will reveal
to you the "commonly known trade sources" for the
many thousands of journals and other materials under
copyright so that you might acquire them. In essence,
by the middle of 1977, there will have to be developed a complete implementation plan - not just by ALA -
but by all of the major associations for libraries in
order to complete these tasks and have libraries
ready to comply - not just with the letter, but with
the spirit of the new copyright law by January 1,
1978. We can comply with both the letter and the
spirit of the law and still provide the levels of
service that we have provided in the past and that we
have said we would like to provide in the future.

RICHARD DE GENNARO

THE MAJOR RESEARCH LIBRARY AND THE NEW COPYRIGHT ACT

I am here speaking as a research librarian and offering my own points of view based on my own practical experience. Everyone says there are no ready answers to these problems, but nevertheless those of us who are working out in the field have to find answers and make decisions. And that is what I am going to try to do.

But before I begin my prepared remarks, I just wanted to do a minisermon for you in response to the one you got yesterday. Yesterday the learned attorney for the publishers told you in no uncertain terms that it was your patriotic duty to mend your sinful eays, to conduct yourselves and your libraries in such a way as to keep the publishers profitable and thereby to help stem the spread of foreign ideologies to these shores, to save the free enterprise system, the American way of life, your mom's apple pie, and my mama's right to serve spaghetti on Sunday and Thursday of every week. I'll bet you never thought you had either the power or the responsibility to shoulder these heavy burdens. Well, I don't think you have. Today I'm going to preach a different doctrine to you. My message to you is more modest. I would have you go forth and obey the new copyright law that was passed by the elders in Congress and signed by your Great White Father who camps on the Potomac.

Director of Libraries, University of Pennsylvania, and Past President, Association of Research Libraries.

That's my simple message - to take the law to your hearts and obey it, no more, no less. Western civilization may fall and capitalism may give way to that other economic system which Mrs. Linden dreads to call by its true name and therefore euphemistically refers to as socialism. All of these terrible things may happen, but if they do, it will not be because of the workings of the new copyright law and it will not be your fault.

Now, let me say from the outset that I do not believe that the new copyright law will seriously affect our libraries' capacity to continue to serve their users in the usual way. There are other trends that concern me deeply, such as escalating book and journal prices, increasing personnel costs, and declining budgets. In comparison to these, the possible harmful effects of the new copyright law are relatively insignificant. I'm somewhat surprised and puzzled at the extent of the interest and concern that librarians have shown about some early versions of Section 108 g, but I believe the final version and the CONTU guidelines are reasonably fair to authors, to publishers, and to librarians, and I can foresee no real difficulties in complying with it. I don't think that ordinary working librarians should feel the need to master all the legal intricacies of the new law and to make elaborate preparations to implement it. To tell the truth, when I first heard about this conference on copyright, I was a little surprised that it was being held at all. I was afraid that the presentations might be postmortems on an issue that I felt had been effectively resolved with the passage of the new law. Copyright was no longer a critical issue for me, and I was prepared to turn my attention to other, more pressing matters. When I received Herb White's letter asking me to present the view of a research librarian, I called to beg off, but ended up by allowing him to persuade me to come here and share my views on the possible effects that the new law might have on libraries and publishers In addition, I thought it would be a good opportunity, while I was here, to urge librarians to continue to freely exercise all the rights that the new law allows and not to permit themselves to be bullied or bamboozled by certain publishers into buying copying privileges which they have always had and which the new law reconfirms.

The other important thing I would like to do is to
try to dispel some of the unrealistic fears and hopes
that many librarians and publishers have about the
either beneficial or harmful effects which increasing
interlibrary loan, networking, and other resource-sharing mechanisms will have on their finances and their
operations. Some publishers fear that library resource-
sharing will seriously diminish their profits. Some librarians hope it will save them from the crunch that is
coming. Both views are, in my opinion, exaggerated. I'll
give my reasons later, but first let me give you some
perspectives on the effect of the new law on research
libraries and publishers, as I see it.

I found the special November 15 issue of the ALA
Washington Newsletter on the new copyright law which
Bob Wedgeworth referred to earlier, to be a handy and
reliable guide through the complexities of the law. It
contains brief highlights of the new law, a librarian's
guide to it, preparations for compliance, and excerpts
from the law and the Congressional Reports, including
the CONTU guidelines. I've read most of what seems to be
of interest and use to a working library administrator,
and several things stood out. I won't get into the details of this, because you've already heard a very fine
presentation from Bob Wedgeworth.

In the new law, the fair use doctrine is given statutory recognition for the first time in Section 107.
Section 108 defines the conditions and limitations under
which libraries can make copies for their internal use
and for interlibrary loans. Nothing in Section 108 limits the library's right to fair use of copyrighted works.
The new law reconfirms most of the rights librarians had
and even extends some. It prohibits "systematic copying,"
but this is no problem since most libraries do not engage in systematic copying in any case. Librarians are
not liable for unsupervised use of photocopying machines
by the public, provided certain conditions are observed.
This is no change from the existing situation. The most
serious limitation on librarians appears in the guidelines which enjoin them from copying more than five articles a year from the last five years of a periodical
title for interlibrary loan purposes. It also stipulates
that libraries have to maintain records to document this

use, and places responsibility for monitoring it on the requesting library.

Well, let's look at these limitations to see what they really mean in practical terms. The limitation of five copies will not seriously interfere with our present interlibrary loan operation. Why not? Because, as we've been trying to tell the publishers for the last several years, most photocopying of journal articles is concentrated among a very small number of the most used titles, many of which are owned by the requesting library, but which for one reason or another are not available. Those titles that we own are exempted from the limitation. The pattern of photocopying of journal articles is the same as that for the use of journals in general, and statistics show that it is a Bradford-type distribution in which, in a large universe of titles, most of the use is concentrated in a relatively small number. Let me give a few actual illustrations using statistics gathered in my own library and at Cornell.

According to the CONTU guidelines, a library may receive five copies per calendar year of articles from any one journal without copyright infringement. This limit applies only to articles published within five years of the request date. From July 1, 1976 to April 1, 1977, our experience at the main library at Penn is as follows: articles were requested from only 182 different copyrighted journals published during the last five years. There was only one journal from which more than five articles were requested. This was a commercial journal in the field of synthetic organic chemistry, and seven articles were ordered from it, several by the same person. There were only four journals from which five articles were requested. These were *Fisica* from Yugoslavia, hardly a hot copyright item; *Journal of Electron Analytical Chemistry*, which is published by Elsevier, presumably a hot item; *The Swedish Journal of Economics*, Stockholm; and *World View*, published by the Council on Religion and International Affairs in New York. There were 138 journals from which only one article was requested, and this is 76 percent of the total number of items requested. For the fiscal year 1975-76, there was a total of 1,062 filled photoduplication requests for Penn patrons of which 10 percent were non-

periodical materials. Let me put these numbers in perspective. Last year we circulated nearly a half-million
volumes to our patrons and we don't circulate periodical
volumes. This is strictly monographs. The periodical use
is in the library and is not measured. We lent 7,700
volumes on interlibrary loan and borrowed only 2,900. We
filled a total of 7,700 photocopy requests in lieu of
interlibrary loan and received 3,700 in return. My purpose in giving you these statistics is to show that the
total amount of photocopying and interlibrary loan traffic in general, and in copyrighted materials in particular, is and will remain a relatively small, almost insignificant, fraction of our total use. Last year we
spent $1.3 million on books and journals, and we would
spend twice that amount if we could get it. We save virtually nothing by using interlibrary loan. We merely obtain some important material for a small number of users
who would otherwise have done without.

The Cornell experience with the five-copy limit is
similar to ours. Madeline Cohen Oakley, the Cornell
Interlibrary Loan Librarian, writes in the *Cornell Bul-
letin* as follows:

The new restrictions on photocopying pose a number of
questions of policy and procedure for Cornell interlibrary loan operations. Although the five articles
per journal photocopy limit may seem low, our experience in interlibrary borrowing (the term covers both
requests for loans and photocopy) at Olin Library has
not, for the most part, borne this out. We consider a
journal for which we have four or more photocopy requests to be "frequently ordered," and all such journals are considered for purchase. To give an example:
In the 1975-76 Fiscal Year, out of a total of 188
different journal titles represented in one group of
requests, only 15 involved multiple copies of four or
more from one journal. Of those 15, nine were for
more than five articles.

She goes on to say that the five-copy limit is likely
to be a problem when a single individual or research
project requires a number of articles from one journal,
and this is also our view at Penn. In those cases some re-

strictions will have to be worked out, and our users
will have to be more selective in what they request.
In those few cases in which we need to exceed the five-
copy limit we can presumably choose to pay a reasonable
royalty to the publisher through the clearinghouse, or
to do without. The mechanism for paying such fees may be
in place by next year. Ben Weil of Exxon, who is attend-
ing this conference, has been appointed to serve as program director of the AAP/TSM Payment Copy Center Task
Force, which is expected to design and implement a payment system by January 1, 1978. He described the concept
in comments from the floor yesterday. The copy center
would periodically invoice the user and allocate the
payment, less its processing charge, to the appropriate
publisher. I wish the center luck, but my guess is that
the processing charges will far exceed the royalty payments.

I would like to urge librarians to exercise all of
the rights and privileges that the new law allows, and
not be inhibited by an exaggerated or misplaced sense of
fair play and justice. Even the Internal Revenue Service
encourages us suffering taxpayers to take all of the de-
ductions to which we are entitled, and to pay no more
taxes than the law requires. Some libraries are already
going to great lengths to establish elaborate procedures
and guidelines, which are far more restrictive than the
law requires, in order to demonstrate their intent to
comply with the spirit as well as the letter of the law
and to show their good faith. By so doing, they run the
risk of losing the rights they are too cautious to exercise. By contrast, some publishers are going to great
lengths to misrepresent the new law to librarians and to
sell them copying privileges which the law gives as a
right.

Let me cite a specific example, an advertising letter
from Robert Maxwell, president of Pergamon Press Inc.,
to his customers. It's dated November 1976 and it goes
like this: "The easy way to comply with the new U.S.
Government Copyright Law." "Dear Subscriber: We enclose
here gratis a microfiche copy of the United States Copyright Law. Under the new law, with certain limited single copy exceptions, it continues to be illegal for any
organization or individual to make xerox or other copies

or to put into data banks, or otherwise reproduce copyright material." That's what he says. "In fact, the new
law, Section 108 now expressly prohibits systematic reproduction or distribution by libraries of single or
multiple copies of journal articles even within their
organization. It also prohibits interlibrary arrangements that substitute for subscriptions, and guidelines
have been promulgated, prohibiting libraries from supplying six or more copies of articles from the same
journal to other libraries in any calendar year."

The letter goes on to offer subscribers the opportunity to purchase a combined subscription, i.e., hard
copy and microform, which gives the subscriber the un-
limited right to reproduce the material for use within
his organization but not for resale. It concludes,
"Won't you please consider ordering a combination rate,
and thus obtain the right to free reproduction while
complying with the new copyright law?"

John Lorenz, the Executive Director of ARL, took Mr.
Maxwell to task for several misstatements and misinterpretations on the new law and the guidelines in the
letter to Pergamon subscribers, and he received the
following brief response:

It was most kind of you to trouble to write to me
the way you did about the misinterpretations and misstatements contained in my first paragraphs relating
to the new copyright act. This was drafted by our
Counsel. However, I must accept the responsibility
for it, and I will be more careful in the future.

And so it goes with the publishers and the librarians.

One more point on this exchange, and now I read from
the ALA *Washington Newsletter* Special Issue. It says:

Section 108 f-4 states that the rights of reproduction
granted libraries by Section 108 do not override any
contractual obligations assumed by the library at the
time it obtained a work for its collections. In view
of this provision, libraries must be especially sensitive to the conditions under which they purchase
materials, and, before executing an agreement which

would limit their rights under the copyright law,
should consult with their legal counsel.

I think you can make the connection back to the Maxwell
letter.

Now I want to talk about library cooperation and inflation. Resource-sharing and networking give librarians
hope and publishers nightmares, but both groups are seriously overestimating the effects the new copyright law
will have on these developments. I believe the economic
trends and forces that are at work today are far more
significant, powerful, and complex than we imagine. Current thinking on copyright and royalties will surely be
overshadowed and overtaken by coming developments.

Libraries are cutting their expenditures for books
and journals because they do not have the funds to buy
them, and not because they're able to get them on interlibrary loan or from the Center for Research Libraries
or the British Library Lending Division. Publishers have
the idea that if they can discourage interlibrary loan
and photocopying, libraries will be forced to spend more
money to buy more books and journals. This is bunk. Libraries can't spend money they don't have. The fact is,
that with or without an effective sharing mechanism and
with rising prices and declining budgets, libraries simply do not have the money to maintain their previous
acquisitions levels. If we cannot afford to buy the materials users need, and if the law prohibits us from
borrowing or photocopying what we don't have, our users
will simply have to do without.

Furthermore, there is an increasing realization that
librarians and scholars alike have developed highly exaggerated notions of the size and range of the library
collections that are actually needed by most library
users.

We know that in general roughly eighty percent of the
demands on a library can be satisfied by twenty percent
of the collection. The Bradford Zipf distributions show
that a small number of journal titles account for a
large percentage of the use. Eugene Garfield's numerous
studies at the Institute for Scientific Information and
his *Journal Citation Reports* bear this out. A University
of Pittsburgh Library School study by Allen Kent and

others found that fifty percent of one library's collection was never used, not even once in a recent four-year period. Herman Fussler's *Patterns and the Use of Books in Large Research Libraries* showed similar use patterns.

In sum, we know that we can satisfy a large proportion of the real needs of our users with a relatively small percentage of our present library collections, and that many of the things that we buy are merely to satisfy the status needs of certain faculty members and librarians. When the budget crunch comes to a library, many of these status purchases will be foregone or dropped and the essentials will be maintained. We will not rely on interlibrary loan or a National Periodicals Library to obtain these missing items. Why not? Because we never needed them in the first place, contrary to the fear of the publishers, for they are rarely, if ever, used. Libraries will continue to buy and stock as many of the high-use books and journals as they can possibly afford.

Incidentally, it is also worth noting that the word "research" is vastly overused in reference to what our faculties do and our libraries support. This is another legacy of the affluent 1960s, when there was seemingly no end to the growth of academia and the increasing numbers of faculty, Ph.D.s, and the wide variety of their needs and interests. The reality now seems to be different. The primary mission of all but a small number of academic libraries should be to support the instructional needs of the students and faculty. To document this, I'll quote from the 1975 Ladd-Lipset survey entitled: "How Professors Spend Their Time," as reported in the *Chronicle of Higher Education* (October 14, 1975, page 2).

The popular assumption has been that American academics are a body of scholars who do their research and then report their findings to the intellectual or scientific communities. Many faculties behave in this fashion, but that overall description of the profession is seriously flawed. Most academics think of themselves as teachers and professionals, not as scholars and intellectuals, and they perform accordingly. Although data on the number of scholarly articles and academic books published each year testify that faculty members are producing a prodigious vol-

ume of printed words, this torrent is gushing forth
from relatively few pens. Over half of all full-time
faculty members have never written or edited any sort
of book alone or in collaboration with others. More
than one-third have never published an article. Half
of the professoriate have not published anything or
had anything accepted for publication in the last two
years. More than one-quarter of all full-time academics have never published a scholarly word.

They summarize, "American academics constitute a
teaching profession, not a scholarly one. There is a
small scholarly sub-group located disproportionately at
a small number of research oriented universities." (When
I use this information at home, I always say that of
course Penn is one of them - and so is Indiana.)

As for the publishers, they may make themselves feel
better by blaming journal cancellations and the dimin-
ishing of orders for books on increasingly effective library resource-sharing via systematic photocopying and
interlibrary loan, rather than on inflation and declining library budgets, but they will be kidding themselves

Resource-sharing will not seriously erode publishers'
profits nor will it help libraries as much as they think
Interlibrary loan is and will continue to be a very small
percentage of total library use. The cost of interlibrary
loan and the demands of library users will not permit it
to grow into something major. Its importance will be in
the capability for delivery more than in the actual use
of that capability. Like the Center for Research Libraries, interlibrary loan is an insurance policy. We do not
justify our annual membership fee in the Center for Research Libraries by the number of things we borrow every
year, but by the amount of purchases we are able to fore-
go by knowing that they are available if and when they
are needed. It is "a penny saved is a penny earned" kind
of economics.

Librarians are naive if they count on their regional
cooperative resource-sharing networks or a National Periodicals Library for major real savings or to weather the
rough times ahead. This is as true for the small college
library consortia as it is for the prestigious research
libraries group. All consortia members are equally vul-

nerable because the magnitude of the cuts they will have
to make to counter inflation and declining support will
play havoc with their sharing plans and will far out-
weigh the minor economies that cooperation and networks
will really yield in the end. In fact, like many automation projects, consortia may be actually costing their
members more than they save if the very substantial cost
of their staff time in making them work is included. The
easy victories come early and cheaply in cooperation.
But what do we do that is cost effective after we've
saved a few positions by joining OCLC and agreed to reciprocal borrowing privileges with our neighbors? What
do we do for an encore after we've reduced our staff,
journal subscriptions, and book intake by five or ten
percent through cooperation and improved management?

The utility of the consortia is not that they will
permit libraries to reduce expenditures on books and
journals so that the money can be used for other library
purposes but that it will permit them to reallocate
their expenditures and reduce their collecting commitments with less damage to their total resources and services than would otherwise have been the case. They are
the same kind of savings that I make when I decide to
vacation at home because I did not have the money to begin with. Inflation is a powerful force, more powerful
than library cooperation or exchanging photocopies of
journal articles. It is inflation that has caused a ten
percent decrease in the median number of volumes added
to ARL libraries last year, along with a five percent
decrease in the number of staff employed.

Let me conclude by saying that research libraries are
quite ready to abide by the new copyright law and to pay
royalties to a National Periodicals Library or to a Publisher's Clearinghouse where the law requires it. However, I believe that the amount and kind of copying that
will be done will not require the payment of any significant amount of royalties and that the dollar amounts
involved will be trivial to both publishers and library
users alike. I think that time and experience will show
that the whole publisher-librarian controversy over
copyright, interlibrary loan, and photocopying was a result of fear and misunderstanding - largely on the part
of the publishers.

Academic libraries are sharing the financial troubles of their parent institutions. These troubles come from long-term economic, social, and demographic trends and they will probably get worse in the years ahead. The troubles that publishers have are caused by changing market forces, and not by library photocopying or deficiencies in the copyright law, and they will not be resolved by the payment of royalties on a few journal articles. My message to publishers is that librarians no longer have the funds to support them in the style to which they became accustomed in the relatively affluent 1960s. My message to librarians is that whatever modest savings we make through networking, cooperation, and resource-sharing in the next several years will be quickly absorbed by the rampant inflation in book and journal prices and rising personnel costs. The fact is, we can no longer afford to maintain the collection, staffing, and service levels that we and our clients have come to expect in the last decade or two. We are suffering a substantial loss in our standard of living. We can rail against it and search for scapegoats, but it would be better if we came to terms with this painful reality and began to scale down our commitments and expectations to match our resources.

DISCUSSION

James Cruse (University of Michigan): I wanted to make one comment and then ask a question. We also did a study of our interlibrary loan requests over the past two years to see how we were in compliance with the new rule, and we discovered essentially the same things. In almost every case we were asking for only two or three copies of articles within the last five years, and in the cases when we had requested more than five (there had only been four instances), they had each been for a specific professor, so that it hadn't been spread out over a number of people and requests. My question concerns the points that we've been talking about both yesterday and today, the fact

that compliance with the law rests on the requesting
library. However, I believe there is something and I
can't quote the section or the part of the law that
indicates that a supplying library has some responsibility for compliance if they believe that the libraries requesting from them are in excess of the proper
number. Would you care to comment on this, and is
there anything that we have to do or should be looking
for in this respect?

Richard De Gennaro: Well, I'm a reasonably intelligent
and attentive guy and I read the ALA *Washington Newsletter* and I didn't see anything like that in there.
Maybe Bob or others can comment on it, but I wouldn't;
certainly in my own situation I wouldn't take that
kind of responsibility. As far as I can see what the
law says is that the responsibility is on the re-
quester and not on the furnisher, and that's good
enough for me. Bob, do you want to clarify this?

Robert Wedgeworth: Well, the section which speaks specifically to that question is contained in the photocopying guidelines and point number four says that
"the requesting entity shall maintain records of all
requests made by it for copies of photorecords of any
materials to which these guidelines apply, and shall
maintain records of the fulfillment of such requests,
which records shall be retained until the end of the
third complete calendar year after the end of the
calendar year in which the respective requests shall
have been made." This is the specific provision. Our
advice to you is that it is simply the responsibility
of the supplying library to be sure that it has a request which formally acknowledges that it is in compliance with the copyright law. The law does cover
the supplying entity, but it's a transfer of liability in this case and I would say that this is very
similar to Section 108 g-1 which requires a library to
be aware, as in the illustration I gave, that two or
three people may want the same article whether they
come in three weeks apart. There is a limit to the
practicality that you can apply to that kind of request and the important thing is to have the evidence
in your file that the library did request it in com-

pliance with the law, in which case you can invoke,
is it in Section 504, I believe, where it says that
. . . ?

Richard De Gennaro: I refuse to become an expert on the
copyright law.

Robert Wedgeworth: Well, the section in which it says
that if a library does something in good faith with
respect to the law then it shall be removed from the
statutory liability.

Nevin Raber (Indiana University): In looking through the
materials I don't find any reference to the teacher
providing the librarian with a large stack of photocopies to put on reserve, none of which have been
stamped that any release has been obtained. What
would be your position if you received such a large
stack of material?

Richard De Gennaro: I don't really know. I think that
we'd somehow turn the person away. I really mean it
when I say that I think we should comply with the law
as best we can and as best we can understand the complicated thing. But it's going to be very difficult.
It's a complex law. I'm not advocating that we take
anything away from the publishers or the authors that
rightfully belongs to them, but on the other hand I'm
saying that we should not have to prove that we're
living within the spirit of the law beyond any shadow
of a doubt, and all that kind of thing. All we can do
is try to live within the law as best we can, and
cope with these matters on an ad hoc basis.

Theodora Andrews (Pharmacy Librarian, Purdue University):
While in general I agree with what you've said, Mr. De
Gennaro, there is one point that bothers me a little
bit. I don't have good statistics for it, but I do believe that in a library like ours where we hold rather
unique materials (pharmaceutical materials are not
widely held, except by a few pharmacy schools and the
pharmaceutical industry), we lend a great deal of material, the same title over and over to pharmaceutical
industries. They have large unique collections too,
but they often don't hold their stock very far back.

I have some feeling, and perhaps Efren Gonzales may comment on this, that with this kind of a situation there will be a great many times where they will run over six copies per year from the same title. I agree there's not going to be a great deal of money involved, but I suspect that with the kind of research they do that they absolutely have to have that material.

Richard De Gennaro: Oh, I wouldn't need a copyright law to put a stop to that. I'd simply tell the commercial pharmaceutical house to buy the journal.

Theodora Andrews: Well, they're willing to, but they probably don't ask for them.

Richard De Gennaro: Why should you lend it to them? I mean, if it's the same journal over and over again, write them and tell them to subscribe.

Theodora Andrews: Yes, but six times a year is not very many.

Richard De Gennaro: Six times a year *is* very many. I think it really is.

Theodora Andrews: I say I hope there's no comment on this, because I have not really sat down and counted this up, but I feel that the number of items we send to them . . .

Richard De Gennaro: If you ever figured your own costs for doing that reproducing and . . .

Theodora Andrews: I've thought about it. I think about it every now and then.

Richard De Gennaro: . . . sending it out to them, it's certainly worth the subscription price to them. In that case I'm on the publisher's side 100 percent. I'd make them buy it.

Theodora Andrews: Well, we do cooperate and we don't like to be difficult about this. As I say these are fairly unique materials, but there are several industries in Indiana that are very, very large borrowers. I believe they sometimes use the materials more than we do.

Richard De Gennaro: As one group of commercial people against another, I really think I'd be on the side of the publishers in insisting that they subscribe.

Jerome Miller (University of Illinois): I'd like to respond to the question about copies of articles being placed on reserve, and I assume the gentleman meant multiple copies of the same article. I recently attended a copyright conference in which this question arose and Eugene Lindenkopf, a copyright attorney in private practice, responded. He said, "Do you view this as making multiple copies in lieu of classroom distribution?" And the individual said, "Yes, we make three copies of an article to place on reserve in lieu of making thirty copies to distribute to students." And then he went back to the committee report and he said, "Well, now, if you look at the teacher's guidelines, they may make multiple copies under certain circumstances for class distribution. If you view this as being in lieu of class distribution, go ahead and make the copies."

T H E V I E W S
EFREN GONZALEZ   O F A S P E C I A L
L I B R A R I A N

While listening to the papers presented at the first
session of this conference, I began to write down some
of the statements I heard that just cried out for rebut-
tal. Commenting on these may be meaningful for all of
us, because regardless of what my personal experience
has been with the development of the new copyright law,
it wasn't your personal experience, and the only thing
we have in common in the sense of that legislation at
this given moment is what has been presented so far in
the proceedings of this conference. So I'd like to make
some comments on what we have all heard presented here.

One of the statements which would have struck a particular note to any member of the Special Libraries Association who had been involved with the legislative
process that took place was the comment of Mr. Brennan's,
a rather cavalier comment I might add, that the library
community did not find it convenient to assist the Senate committee when it was developing its report in the
area of interlibrary loan. Now as with many other things
you have heard in this conference, I'm hoping that you

Manager, Technical Information Services, Bristol-
Myers Company, and Past President, Special Libraries Association. Substituting for Frank McKenna, Executive Director, Special Libraries Association, unable to attend
because of illness.

will not assume because it was said that it was so. In
this instance it certainly was not so.

The Special Libraries Association, as were all the
other associations that have been active in the effort
of assisting the legislation through Congress, was indeed a participant in the hearings, an invited participant in the hearings before the Senate subcommittee at
which all of the library associations commented on the
law as it then stood. Having done that and, incidentally, having made no particular comment about the Section
108 g-2 or any of those sections that have developed so
much interest since then, I found after the hearings
were over, after the hearing opportunities were closed
by the Senate subcommittee, that the Senate report passing the bill on contained some incredible interpreta-
tions, including the now interesting and famous systematic photocopying concept.

The Senate report stated correctly that there was no
definition in the law, nor could they supply a definition of what "systematic photocopying" meant. So, in order to overcome that problem, they proceeded to list
six, I believe it was, specific examples of what they
considered to be systematic photocopying, and that document is the one that Mr. Brennan urged you all to read.
I certainly urge you to do the same, except that I also
urge you to read what happened after that, which describes the main effort made by the library associations
to overcome what we all considered to be an unwarranted
interpretation of a word or words or phrase that admittedly was not defined in the first place. For that reason, it is not sufficient to read the Senate report on
the bill. You must read the House report and the conference report on it, as well. You must bear in mind that
the conference report represents the ultimate decision
of the Senate as well as of the House. It is a compromise, what both houses of Congress agreed to, and it is
true that, as Mr. Brennan pointed out, it is not sufficient merely to read the law. One must read the legislative history consisting of all the testimony and all
the reports, and I think I should add to that what he
did not, that the chronological sequence of the legislative history is not, as I understand it, very impor-

tant. That is to say, it is the law's most recent history that tends to have the most weight.

You might ask me why and where. And the answer is, in the courts. Furthermore, as Mr. Baumgarten indicated, enforcement of this law is a matter among the parties that are affected. We do not have the FTC or the FDA or the IRS or any other agency in the government that is going to enforce this law. The parties involved are going to enforce the law with lawsuits as the ultimate enforcement mechanism if they cannot agree on alternative guidelines or other mechanisms by which they will come to grips with it.

I was impressed also by Mr. Burchinal's statement that two-thirds of the federal research dollars, in terms of the reports on that research, goes into privately owned journals. Of course he was not speaking for the private sector of the country, but I think it is important to remember that virtually all the research published for public consumption which is not secret or company confidential material also goes into these privately owned journals. Few organizations that do research can afford to or care to support a research journal that is publicly circulated. All of those dollars flow to the journal owners, whether they be societies or whether they be commercial organizations. I find this interesting, incidentally, from the point of view of a company, or for that matter of a government contractor or a government agency.

As for the scientific and technical and medical literature, the employee of a company engaged in research is expected to publish the results of certain of his or her work. The company also pays for any cost of such publication, specifically the page charges. The company also pays for the subscription to the journal in which this report and others are published. The same company also pays for a library or information center to make this material available to the employee. It also pays for the photocopying and any other costs required in the information transfer process. Now that company is being told that there are certain circumstances under which it will have to pay fees to the copyright holder in order to make copies beyond a certain level.

There is an area in the law, if you include the
guidelines CONTU has been able to put together by almos
general agreement of all parties, where photocopying
fees are specifically implied. Such fees are not required under the CONTU guidelines, but there is the assumption that some mechanism will be devised by which
additional copies over the specified maximum of five
will require payment to the copyright owner. However, w
find ourselves now with a mechanism suggested by the As
sociation of American Publishers that even goes beyond
the question of interlibrary loan to take into account
copies made within the company organization by the library and any copies made on unsupervised machines within the organization. Although we have yet to find out
how we are all going to comply with the so-called CONTU
guidelines which are especially designed for interlibrary photocopying, already we are being presented
with a mechanism that goes far beyond that set of guidelines. This was developed, as I understand it, by the
AAP and the Information Industry Association special
task force, a joint effort that took many drafts; yet i
was not presented to CONTU on March 31 by both groups,
only by the Association of American Publishers. I'm not
quite sure why that withdrawal by IIA occurred, but it
puzzles me. We have a mechanism that has been presented
CONTU asked for that mechanism because the publishers,
at meeting after meeting, had been suggesting that they
needed one. They finally were told, "Well, tell us what
it is." And now Mr. Koch tells us that what they have
presented is merely a draft. So I am confused. I hope
you're not, but I am confused about what that document
represents and whom it represents. I may be wrong, but
my impression is that the clearinghouse mechanism is being presented by the people who drafted it and not necessarily by the entire membership of AAP. That is, has
this mechanism been tested by the members of the publishing industry to determine whether or not it really represents something most publishers can live with or wish
to live with?

Certainly Bella Linden's presentation made it clear
that her clients were not happy with the mechanism as
presented. The Authors League, through Irwin Karp, also
indicated that it too was unhappy with the AAP's pro-

posal, as they did at the CONTU meeting where it was
presented. It seems to me that inasmuch as the Authors
League and the clients whom Bella Linden represents do
not approve of the way in which the mechanism was developed, since it was done without consulting them, that
the library community could take the same approach.

Let me put it positively. I feel that what we should
do is encourage those who wish to collect the money to
present us with something reasonable to look at, something representative of the publishing community as a
whole for us to examine. My impression is that the six
library associations that have dealt together with the
copyright issue are trying to do exactly that. As a
matter of fact Mr. Frase has indicated that although
the library associations have postponed some testimony
for CONTU tentatively planned for this summer, primarily because they wish to see what they will be dealing
with. I'm hoping that the proposed clearinghouse mechanism will have a clearer base of operations, a clearer
understanding of what it is it represents. Does it represent a few publishers? Does it represent many publishers? Are other publishers going to present different
mechanisms for payment? Are there other guidelines that
will be needed? I am in agreement with much of what De
Gennaro advises. We should respond, and we should do
what is necessary to be done. Let those who need to develop mechanisms and guidelines; let those who are interested in collecting our money present us with what
they agree is a good way to do that; and then let us
comment on their proposals.

That there is a need for input from the library community to those people is obvious. I think that they
always have had access to the library community, especially through the Council of National Library Associations. Somebody earlier on mentioned who those library
associations are; I'll repeat their names: the American
Association of Law Libraries, the American Library Association, the Association of Research Libraries, the
Medical Library Association, the Music Library Association, and the Special Libraries Association. The six
library associations, through their representatives,
constitute an ad hoc committee of the council, which I
hope will continue to work together in this interpreta-

tive phase as they did so successfully in the legislative phase. After having worked together ad hoc through to the point of the completion of the legislation, the Council of National Library Associations has asked the members of the committee to continue as a group, to continue working on actual practices and implementation under the law. Let's see if we can't work together as community, special, public, university libraries to seek the interactions that are necessary among ourselves to present a unified position in response to anything which is proposed for us to work with.

In response to a question, Bella Linden suggested that the publishing community cannot make any money on a clearinghouse for at least five years. Now it's not her money obviously, it's our money she's talking about, and if no effective income to publishers is anticipated for five years during which we are paying that clearinghouse, it seems to me that the whole concept needs rethinking. Paying our money for their principle is something which we ought to investigate thoroughly before we start paying them. If indeed there is no evidence that the clearinghouse will have a favorable impact on publisher revenues, I see no reason why we should agree to participate in such a clearinghouse. It seems to me that the clearinghouse must be something reasonable. Creating a mechanism in the technical sense is only part of the problem. The real problem is whether or not there is useful income that the publisher or other holder of the copyright will benefit from as a result of our using that mechanism. The five years with no payout that Bella Linden estimates worries me greatly, because all during that time to what purpose will we have been supplying money?

Something else that was mentioned yesterday provides another interesting problem. Throughout most of the negotiations and discussions with publisher representatives and author representatives, the library community has turned back to the question, "How do you determine the difference between a technical publication and a nontechnical publication?" Publishers have insisted many times that this new mechanism is based primarily on the assumption that only the scientific, technical, and medical publications would be immediately involved. No definition has yet been developed to tell us how to know which kinds of publications are what. We also know that regardless of what kind of library we work in, we are not universally limited to a certain type of publication. Our patrons cross over, whether we're in a university setting or an industrial setting. Mrs. Linden made the point that you cannot separate publishers on that basis either. There seems to be some disagreement in that area as to whether or not the mechanism ought to be limited just to technical publications. How would that affect publishers? Would they have some journals within the mechanism and some journals outside? The near disaster of NTIS copyright that Mr. Zurkowski mentioned was something that the Special Libraries Association objected to strenuously in writing at the time, and as you know, the conference committee report on this bill, while it adopted virtually all of the House version of the bill, adopted the Senate version of the bill with regard to this question. I think we have a chance now to see the full implications of what was being proposed at essentially the eleventh hour. I was going to quote the Pergamon Press letter, but Dick De Gennaro got there ahead of me. It is extraordinary and an example of what publishers, if left to their own devices, may conjure up for us.

Those of you who are not in the medical field may not be knowledgeable about the Williams and Wilkins case. In the midst of that brouhaha, right after the hearing examiner said he felt that Williams and Wilkins was the winner, which later turned out not to be the case, Williams and Wilkins announced their new subscription rates for the coming year. What they did in their proposal was to say that for a slight increase in fee, a subscriber would have the right to make photocopies with the following exceptions: photocopying had to be done on your premises; it could not be done for someone in your company who was not on your premises; it could not be done for another library for interlibrary loan. That proposal leads you very quickly to the conclusion that the only way you can get a copy of any of their journal articles is to subscribe to all their journals, because you would be unable to get what you needed through interlibrary

loan. This ploy did not survive by the tests of library
hue and cry and Williams and Wilkins withdrew it.

What I want to emphasize is that without some interaction with the library community, it is going to be
very hard for publishers to understand what library operations are. Our conversations with them over the years
are replete with complete misunderstanding. Again, as
Dick De Gennaro suggested, much of this has come about
because the publishers are assuming that there is a gold
mine in photocopying and we don't see it. As a matter of
fact, I suspect most libraries would be glad to get out
of the photocopying business. The only reason we're in
it is because the people who publish the journals cannot
supply the material other than the first time. No one
else is volunteering. Certainly the people who need the
material are not in a position to wander around the
countryside, getting individual permissions or making
individual requests to publishers to submit a single
copy of something. Most publishers do not keep back issues beyond perhaps even a few months in some cases,
certainly not more than a few years. It just seems incredible that all is dependent on so erroneous an assumption.

Now to my notes. I believe that at least from a special library's point of view, there is a continuing attempt, whether purposeful or inadvertent, to bring forward an erroneous concept about libraries in profit-
making organizations that was laid to rest with the issuance of the conference report. Basically, the conference report shows that as long as a library in a profit-
making organization fulfills all of the conditions under Section 108 a, it should be treated just like any
other library with regard to the exemptions available
under Section 108. I would think there are very few libraries, whether profit-making or otherwise, that do
not make their materials available to researchers in the
same field, indeed that are not open to the public, at
least by appointment and certainly through interlibrary
loan. I suspect that the majority of those that are not
are in government organizations, not private industry.
The fact that company libraries often have responsibilities for confidential company classified material is
sheer nonsense. Those materials are not copyrighted in

the first place and are not at issue with regard to availability to the public. It is my hope that the continuing attempts to make a distinction among libraries will be resisted by the entire library community.

For example, the King Study, which is going along under sponsorship of CONTU and NCLIS, includes a question in it as to whether or not you supply copies to a library that is in a profit-making company as opposed to one in a nonprofit organization. I don't believe that is a relevant question. The law does not make such a distinction. As a matter of fact, the Congress went to some pains to erase the distinction that had become such a quarrel with the Senate when it issued its report. Even Mr. Koch, when testifying to CONTU on March 31 and enumerating the features of the new law, included this comment: "Scientific societies will have to recognize these features and take them into account in establishing appropriate procedures for encouraging the continuation of both 'fair-use' photocopying for scholarly purposes without fee, and photocopying for a fee in industrial libraries." Now that's just out of the blue. There is no requirement and no distinction made in the law or in the legislative history that says that libraries in profit-making organizations may be or have to be or can be treated any differently with regard to interlibrary loans and other photocopying exemptions given to any other library under Section 108. The Special Libraries Association does not consist entirely of profit-making organizations. I don't mean to give you that impression, but it turns out that it has tended to become the focal point for these kinds of considerations, and that is why we've placed so much emphasis on it.

On the other hand, I think that the one contribution the Special Libraries Association wants to make, if nothing else, is to emphasize that the way the law developed, the sequence of events leading to the attempt to differentiate between libraries as profit-making and nonprofit organizations has been eliminated in the law's language by the more recent and final conference report. In addition to that, I think that SLA wants very much to maintain the six-library association effort to deal with the emerging implementation problems, to help speak with one voice for the profession, and to resist the fragmentation of the library community which will permit one segment to be played off against another.

I find it hard to reconcile what we all hoped we would hear or learn by coming to this conference with what we actually have heard. On the other hand, during these past two days you have been placed in somewhat the same position that those people who have had the dubious distinction of working with this emerging situa tion have been dealing with over those years it has bee developing. What I have been hearing here is essentiall a deja-vu experience. I remember hearing it in the con- ference of resolution of copyright issues, in testimony before the Senate and before the House. I feel that the library associations' success in this area is really no so much protecting the innocents, as Mr. Wedgeworth sug gested, as a triumph of common sense.

DISCUSSION

Howard Dillon (University of Chicago): Mr. Gonzalez, th document which Mr. Weil has made available to us in- cludes this wording on page 4 at the bottom in the section called Fair Use and Related Copying: "Publis ers interested in the CPC based programs have gener- ally indicated that they will accept this fair use copying, either the on site making or the requesting of another library of the number of copies and under conditions spelled out in the CONTU guidelines for photocopying through interlibrary arrangements." The clearinghouse concept is something I've only heard about in the last two days since I am pretty new to this, and I've had trouble figuring out why this clearinghouse was being proposed if, as a library, I follow the CONTU guidelines. If I may request more than five copies of journal articles published more than five years ago from a given title in a year and if my users and I myself follow the fair use copying I can't see that I'll be doing much business with th clearinghouse, which I think is perhaps what you wer saying as well. But I'm really inviting you or some-

one, before I leave today, to help me understand from
where the publishers think this volume of business
will come. Are they looking at libraries as the principal purchasers of the service of the clearinghouse
or is it some other individual organization they have
in mind?

Mary Reslock (Dow Chemical Company): May I interrupt for
just a minute?

Efren Gonzalez: Sure.

Mary Reslock: I think my comment might have some bearing
on the same question. I think little attention has
been paid to the cost of record retention. That's a
costly thing if you're going to do it in a systematic
way. What value is there going to be for the clearinghouse if the cost of record retention is going to reveal the fact that many of your titles are rarely
used and you can absorb the cost of record keeping
only by dropping some of your titles?

Efren Gonzalez: Well, the cost that you're referring to
are costs of the library. They will not be passed on
or cannot be passed on, and I'm sure the clearinghouse would refuse to accept those costs. As a matter
of fact, when we sat down to talk about this general
problem in a committee that Paul Zurkowski, by coin-
cidence, was chairing, the librarians pointed out
that the cost of keeping the records and informing
the copy center of its use of copies was an added
cost to that which is already intrinsic in making
photocopies. The publishers refused to accept that
cost as a deduction from the fee, whatever it would
be.

Mary Reslock: I don't think that would be proposed, but
I think that you are gathering statistics on the use-
fulness of many of your titles, and somewhere along
the line costs have to be evened out, and perhaps
you'll be dropping titles which are of greater revenue to the publishers than the royalty payments.

Efren Gonzalez: All of those things seem too painfully
obvious to librarians, but not to publishers. Now for
example, I think it's interesting to note that yes-

terday we had two conflicting comments about how much
is a reasonable copy. Somewhere along the line somebody indicated that some survey would answer the
question. On the other hand, as has been often done,
whenever you get backed into a corner on something as
fundamental as "How much are you going to charge us?"
the publishers immediately stand up and theoretically
leave the room and say "No, we would be in violation
of antitrust if we discussed this together and therefore we can't tell you." Now I don't understand how
anybody can assess whether or not we can afford to
make payments. It's just a fundamental question of
whether we can afford to make payments to a copyright
clearinghouse, because of the numbers of dollars involved. And how we are going to assess whether it's
realistic, if they can't tell us in advance what
they're talking about in terms of dollars?

Bernard Fry: This is not necessarily to points just
made, but I think there has emerged yesterday and today a clear indication of the need for more firm data
and statistics, particularly as Bob Wedgeworth and
also Mr. De Gennaro indicated. There are some studies
under way which have not been mentioned, but which I
think will have a particular impact. One of them is
the ASLIB study in Great Britain that's now under way.
Tony Woodward is carrying it out for the Research and
Development Group. They are rejecting, for example,
the Bradford scattering and concentration idea. They
feel that the main significance lies not in how many
copies of *Science* or *Scientific American* or the very
large circulation journals are borrowed, but rather
copies of those journals which are more or less marginal or which are new journals. They're also tracing
for example, in trying to see whether there's a caus-
al relationship between journals that have been borrowed and whether libraries borrowing those journals
have cancelled. Now this is just one. The MINITEX and
the King reports that the National Commission for Libraries and Information Science and CONTU supported
are very important, but I think that what Dick brought
out earlier, the need is for libraries to keep simple
data with hopefully not too much administrative bur-

den, so that after a year or two years, we will know
much more what we're talking about and we will not be
making a number of assumptions which may or may not
be true. They are being made from our past experience
and I'm not questioning them, but I think that the
absence of firm data is something that we need to consider. We also need to keep abreast of these studies
which are being made only recently, and some of which
are still under way. Just as a footnote I might add
that we here at Indiana University are also engaged
in two studies, one for NSF and one for NEH on the
motivations for cancelling journal subscriptions.
There is a great deal that we do not know and we may
discover some surprising things, but some of the
causes that we're attributing here today may or may
not be borne out.

Elizabeth Smith (Environmental Protection Agency): A lot
of special libraries have been using information bro-
kers as a way of securing photocopies. Does the first
criterion under fair use that it not be made for profit mean that an information broker getting a photocopy at our request would have to pay a fee on each
and every item should the clearinghouse come to be?

Efren Gonzalez: Well, how the information broker gets
his copy to send to you is his problem. The House report says that isolated spontaneous making of a single photocopy by a library in a for-profit organization without any systematic effort to substitute photocopying for subscription or purchase would be covered by Section 108, even though the copies are fur-
nished through the employees of the organization for
use in their work. Similarly, for-profit libraries
could participate in interlibrary arrangements for
exchange of photocopies as long as the production or
distribution was not systematic. These activities by
themselves would ordinarily not be considered "for
direct or indirect commercial advantage." This is
wording from the bill: "Since the advantage referred
to, in this clause, must attach to the immediate commercial motivation behind the reproduction or distribution itself, rather than to the ultimate profit

making motivation behind the enterprise in which the library is located."

James Self (Indiana University): I want to comment on who it is who's likely to be customers of clearing-houses or whatever mechanism is set up. I think that Mr. De Gennaro is right, and that it won't be librar-ies of his type that would be using the clearing-houses. In my own position I work for the regional campuses at Indiana University which are scattered around the state and have much smaller libraries than you find here in Bloomington. There are people on these campuses who are doing fairly sophisticated re-search, so there's a whole office of which I am in charge that, in effect, has as its purpose to exploit the resources of the Bloomington library and there is a lot of photocopying. We've been doing a study of all the campuses, and we've found great differences among them. Some of them will have no problem in staying within five per title per year. But some of them, where there is a satellite medical program, have in the past been using far more than five arti-cles per year from the Bloomington and Indianapolis collections. They don't have money in their book budgets to buy these journals at $500 a subscription. So something's got to change there, and it will have much more of an effect. I think that smaller librar-ies are more dependent upon larger libraries than they realize.

Efren Gonzalez: You may be right. The smaller libraries have smaller collections, but I think that it becomes a management problem. That's why we're so in the dark. Whatever the cost is going to be to make a photocopy beyond what we now have to pay for the mechanics of getting the copy, I mean the additional fee or cost to the copyright holder, is then going to be a question of arithmetic. Is it cheaper to request the photo-copies or to subscribe? Depending on how much money you have to make that decision. . . .

James Self: Or to do without.

Efren Gonzalez: Well, that's often the case.

Ben Weil: The discussion at this meeting of course has
been one of the difficulties of discussing a subject
without having it presented, and there was no opportunity to present the plans, reasons, and so forth
of the AAP program. Consequently, a fair number of
unnecessary misapprehensions have been forthcoming
at this meeting. For example, that IIA is withdrawing
its support for the program, which is not true. It
didn't appear on the statement, because the implementation just for the present is in the hands of AAP.
Secondly, the program has been tested on a good many
journals. You heard a report from a minority publisher, but you heard no report from the majority of publishers, although I think I did mention that so far
we are able to identify some 700 journals of the publishers who are willing to be involved in this system.
I may add, and I'm sure the Indiana study is also
finding out, that a great many of these publishers
will charge nothing. In other words, the option is
left to the publisher, and many of the publishers at
present do not intend to charge for photocopying.
This information will be forthcoming when they tell
you, or when they tell the AAP, and we will include
the information in the list that there is no fee required from these journals. I won't say anything further on this, because there will be opportunities and
presentations both at the ALA meeting and the SLA
meeting. Michael Harris (who chairs the Scientific,
Technical, and Medical Committee of the AAP) is making presentations at both of them. I may add that
this is not a first draft, it is a draft which requires improvement, and in that respect it is a document in which you can expect to see further changes.
However, the document you have is not a first draft.
The program is ongoing and it is intended not to add
to the price of photocopying but to have a charge to
take care of those photocopies which you cannot make
under fair use and which you cannot make under the
CONTU guidelines. The system itself requires you to
do no record keeping. Once you have reported, record
keeping is your own business.

Efren Gonzalez: You say there's no record keeping, but somehow we have to report to the mechanism and there are some records involved.

Ben Weil: Well, you have to do something up to the point of reporting, that's perfectly true, but similarly you don't use a system unless you have to pay, and if you don't have to pay, you don't have to keep any records.

Herbert S. White: This is a point of explanation, and perhaps of apology to Mr. Weil. The AAP proposal developed long after the program for this conference was finalized, and I'm sure you'll recognize, after having been here for the last day and a half, there are no empty spots on this program to allow the insertion of another paper. It turns out, possibly because of the selection of our panelists, that all the ball players in this game were in fact here, starting with CONTU and involving people in the publishing and the author communities who are in favor or opposed. It is perhaps unfortunate that we ended up talking at great length about something which was never formally presented, but I'm glad at least that Ben Weil was able to attend, and at least to bring copies of his proposal. I felt this was the least we could do, but probably also the best we could do.

IMPACT ON EMERGING NETWORKS, CONSORTIA, AND THE NATIONAL PLAN

ALPHONSE TREZZA

Describing the impacts of the revised copyright law on networks, consortia, and the national program is not going to be easy. What the impacts and their magnitude are depend in some measure on how you interpret the law, and that is likely to depend on whom you talk to or what newsletter or publication you read. Nor is the disagreement a simple dichotomy between copyright owners and users of copyrighted materials. Within the publishing community, there is sharp disagreement as to whether or not the compromise on interlibrary loan has "given away the store."

In the library community, you have on one hand a large segment which read the interlibrary loan clause and the CONTU guidelines and said to themselves, "We're home free." However, there are a number of librarians who (probably on the advice of legal counsel) are tearing their hair and moaning that they will have to cut off all kinds of services because they are "systematic." Most library and information people, I suspect, are still trying to make up their minds, or better yet, trying to get someone to give them an authoritative answer as to precisely what the new law means.

I wish I could say that I have the answers to all of their questions, but I don't - and I don't believe any-

Executive Director, National Commission on Libraries and Information Science.

one else has them either. Unfortunately, neither the
law, nor the guidelines, nor the conference report are
either crystal clear or all-inclusive. Some questions
will have to wait for us to gather experience as we operate under the new law, and some may not be resolved
without resorting to lawsuits. There is a great deal,
however, that seems fairly clear - and that we can talk
about.

In the first place, whatever the shortcomings of P.L.
94-553 as finally enacted, it is a far better document
from the point of view of networks and consortia than
was the version passed by the Senate. Without the proviso permitting photocopying for interlibrary loan and
the CONTU guidelines putting the burden of compliance
on the requesting library, the new law could well have
strangled resource sharing, which is a major function
of most networks. As far as the normal flow of shared
resources is concerned, I don't believe that there will
be any measurable effect. All of the data we have and
all of my experience in 28 years as a librarian indicate
that virtually all of the interlibrary loan traffic in
journal articles will be exempt under the guidelines.
Five requests for articles from a given journal in a
single year is usually more than enough to trigger a request for a subscription, if the budget permits, so the
problem is almost self-solving. However, that phrase,
"if the budget permits," looms as a larger factor with
every passing year, and librarians are going to have to
begin looking, if they are not already, at the use, if
any, being made of journals to which they already have
subscriptions. Journals which are not being used or
which are being used only infrequently are going to be
dropped, so that funds can be used for those in demand,
or for interlibrary loan.

While the traffic may not change that much, the procedures are going to have to be changed considerably.
Interlibrary loan librarians are going to have to keep
better records and keep them for far longer than has
been the usual practice. Under the guidelines, the requesting library must certify to the supplying library
that each request is in compliance with the guidelines.
This means that the records of previous requests during
the year must be immediately accessible and filed by

journal title or issue, so that the number of previous requests can be checked quickly. Further, the record of each request must be kept for three full years after the close of the calendar year in which the request was made. If nothing else, this means that some additional storage space will have to be found or some microfilming performed.

On the supplying library side, the procedures are going to have to include a check for the certification of compliance, and some supplying entities are going to want to maintain copies of the certified requests for their own protection. In this case, I am not sure that microfilm would be sufficient, so there is more storage space needed. Consider the problem this poses for a major research library, which fills tens of thousands of requests per year.

There is also the question of what constitutes certification of compliance, or to use the term in the guidelines, representation? Is a check mark in a block sufficient? Or initials? Should there be a provision for indicating that the requesting library has a subscription? For indicating the purpose of the request (e.g., replacement, patron request, etc.), the redesign of the interlibrary loan form should be given careful, deliberate consideration and the widest possible coordination. There are only eight months left to get it designed, approved, printed, and distributed to thousands of libraries in tens of thousands of copies, if it is going to be available for use by January 1, 1978. Networks which are using computers and telecommunications for forwarding requests are also going to have to change their procedures and formats and decide what constitutes representation of compliance, and what additional information they ought to have. Wouldn't it be nice if, in the process, all of the networks got together and devised a standard telecommunications format for interlibrary loan requests? We are going to have to have one sooner or later, so why not now?

It seems clear that the distributive networks and consortia, that is, those based on two-way sharing, can continue to operate, but what about the star and hierarchical configurations, where there is a central source that dispenses without receiving? Remember that the pro-

hibitions against "related or concerted" and "systematic" reproduction are still in the law and still undefined. There is an interesting paragraph in the conference report, which I want to read to you:

> The point has been made that the present practice on
> interlibrary loans and use of photocopies in lieu of
> loans may be supplemented or even largely replaced
> by a system in which one or more agencies or institu-
> tions, public or private, exist for the specific pur-
> pose of providing a central source for photocopies.
> Of course, these guidelines would not apply to such
> a situation.

Now what, precisely, does that paragraph mean? It obviously excludes from the guidelines such operations as
University Microfilms, ISI, and the proposed NTIS service, but they are all operating under licenses anyway.
How does one interpret it with respect to the regional
medical library network, or with the National Library of
Medicine (NLM) as its center, or with respect to the National Commission's proposed periodicals access program?
Would you believe that I can't even get agreement among
my own staff on this question? One can argue that since
NLM has practically the entire universe of medical literature, it almost never needs to borrow, and that the
size and unilateral nature of its photocopying make it
"systematic." Similarly, the "comprehensive periodicals
collection dedicated for lending service" which is presumed for the periodicals access program, exists "for
the specific purpose of photocopying," as described in
the paragraph quoted.

On the other hand, since the regional medical library
network has been around for some 10 years, and NLM has
been providing photocopying for some 25 years before
that, one can argue that they are integral to "present
practice," so they can continue to operate as they do
now. This doesn't help us much on the periodicals access
program, which hasn't started yet. We know the periodicals access program isn't supposed to replace the present system. Its only purpose is to make it more efficient and take the worst of the load off the large research libraries. We still expect that 80 percent of the

requests made will be filled at the local, state, or regional level and that the large research libraries will
still be the resources of last resort for the rare and
esoteric materials. The "comprehensive collection" center is simply an intermediate source and switching point,
so that's all right too. In addition, since the center
is expected to carry multiple subscriptions for heavily
used titles and lend originals when appropriate, it cannot be said that it exists only "for the specific purpose of photocopying." On the other hand, well, you
could go back and forth on this for hours, and we have,
but you see the problem. Since legislation is always the
product of negotiation and compromise, it is seldom une-
quivocal, and one has to use some judgment.

Personally, I don't agree with either the "business
as usual" types or with the "viewers with alarm." To the
first, I point out what I said earlier, that we are going to have to change procedures, that we are going to
have to keep much better records, and that we must become and remain much more aware of what we are doing and
why. To the "viewers with alarm," I point out that it is
inconceivable that Congress intended to hamstring the
exchange of scholarly information or the provision of
information to the public. Let me give you some more
quotes, this time from Public Laws 91-345 and 93-568,
which established the National Commission and authorized
the White House Conference, respectively.

From P.L. 91-345:

Section 2. The Congress hereby affirms that library
and information services adequate to meet the needs
of the people of the United States are essential to
achieve national goals and to utilize most effectively the nation's educational resources and that the
federal government will cooperate with state and local governments and public and private agencies in
assuring optimum provision of such services.

Section 5. Functions
(4) develop overall plans for meeting national library and informational needs and for the coordination of activities at the federal, state, and local
levels, taking into consideration all of the library

and informational resources of the nation to meet
those needs.

From P.L. 93-568:

Whereas the preservation and dissemination of information and ideas are the primary purpose and functio:
of libraries and information centers; and

Whereas the growth and augmentation of the nation's
libraries and information centers are essential if a
Americans are to have reasonable access to adequate
services of libraries and information centers; and

Whereas new achievements in technology offer a poten
tial for enabling libraries and information centers
to serve the public more fully, expeditiously, and
economically.

In view of these stated objectives, I find it hard to
believe that either Congress or the courts are going to
shut off the flow of information.

I should also point out that to a certain extent we
are all working in the dark, with incomplete information. Aside from the uncertainties in the interpretation
of the law, we do not really have complete information
on the volume and patterns of photocopying for interlibrary loan. There have been dozens of studies of various pieces by both librarians and publishers, but no national study performed under conditions acceptable to
both. The photocopy study which King Research is com-
pleting for us now is designed to give us just such an
overall picture, and until we have the final results, I
would caution you not to leap to conclusions about what
the impact of the new law is likely to be.

There is another point which that study brings to
mind. The limitations in the law and the various guidelines are not cutoff points beyond which photocopying is
prohibited. All they establish is the limits below which
no payment to the copyright holder is required. Copies
in excess of the guidelines can be perfectly legal, provided payment is made. The second part of the study,
which is now under way, is the design and feasibility
testing of a royalty payment mechanism. In addition, the

publishers are desperately trying to develop and put
into operation before January 1, 1978, a workable payment mechanism. Lest you think that "desperately" is
too strong, I invite you to consider the position of
the publishers if the new law goes into effect without
such a mechanism in place. If after demanding payment
for photocopying for the last 15 years or so, they fail
to provide the means for doing so, they could - in all
justice - be accused of seriously hampering the flow of
information they purport to promote. Aside from the traditional nonprofit library community, there are thousands of libraries and information centers in private,
for-profit organizations who cannot, or will not, open
their collections to others, and who are ready, willing,
and able to pay for the privilege of photocopying, providing only that there is some reasonable mechanism for
doing so. Are they to be denied the ability to serve
their clientele's needs, or more likely, encouraged to
flout the law? Obviously, the publishers have to do
something, and there is very little time in which to do
it.

The first proposal of the group that is working on
what they call a copy payment center was presented to
the Commission on New Technological Uses of Copyrighted
Works (CONTU) recently. There are a great many unan-
swered questions about the first cut. Unfortunately,
ever since the consent decree on geographic market division a few years ago, everybody in the publishing business is very skittish about possible antitrust actions,
so they are very nervous about almost any cooperative
effort. Partly due to this and partly due to the haste
with which it was prepared, the first proposal leaves
something to be desired. One can infer that publishers
feel the need for additional legislation to provide them
with antitrust protection and an "umbrella statute" to
protect libraries from infringement suits by publishers
who do not participate in the copy payment center plan.
There isn't any likelihood of getting either of these
enacted by January 1, 1978. However, the publishers seem
to be very serious about getting something in place by
January 1. They have obtained the full-time services of
Ben Weil (on leave from Exxon) to push the project to
completion.

I can hear the muttering now from the librarians.
"We can't pay royalties for photocopies; our budgets are
stretched to the limit already." "How can we construct a
budget, when we don't know whether or what we will have
to pay in royalties?" "We will have to stop photocopying
entirely; it's too complicated to keep track of." This
kind of a reaction is a cop-out. Libraries are going to
have to make changes, and some of them may be pretty
drastic, but they don't have to stop functioning. I have
already mentioned the necessity for becoming and remaining more aware of what we are doing and why, with respect to interlibrary loan procedures and records. Let
me suggest that we need a similar awareness with respect
to acquisitions.

From time immemorial, publishers have been coming up
with new journals, and libraries have been subscribing
because the topic of the new journal is "hot" or in demand at the moment. Then the topic fades from popularity,
but the libraries continue to subscribe because they are
reluctant to "break the run." And the journal continues
to be published because there is a "demand," and so on,
ad infinitum and ad nauseum. Journal publishers love library subscriptions because they feel that once they sell
the first subscription, they have the library hooked,
and that is like money in the bank. Until quite recently, this has been largely true. However, as Dick De
Gennaro pointed out in his article in the February 1977
issue of *American Libraries*, inexorable budget pressures are forcing librarians to look more carefully at
their journal subscriptions and cancel those which are
not used. I suggest that the new copyright law is likely
to accelerate this trend. Contrary to the presumed expectation of the publishers that restrictions on photocopying would encourage libraries to buy more subscriptions, the reverse is likely to happen. Libraries are
being forced to look at their acquisitions policies from
the point of view of cost effectiveness and cost/benefit
ratios. Consider that preliminary data from a current
study at the University of Pittsburgh indicates that
over a period of seven years, over half of the collection, including both journals and monographs, was never
used, *not even once*! When you take into account the
costs of acquiring, processing, and storing this unused

material, you find a lot of room for easing up on the
budget. Nor, I suspect, is this phenomenon confined to
the University of Pittsburgh, or even to academic libraries. As librarians become aware of this phenomenon,
and as they begin keeping continuous track of usage and
real demand, they are going to start looking with more
jaundiced eyes at a great many little-used subscriptions.
  There is another factor which must be taken into account here. As the national network evolves from the development of state and regional networks, and in particular, as the national periodicals access program comes
into being, the acquisition of journal articles via
interlibrary loan is going to become a great deal more
assured and much more timely. As this happens, the re-
luctance of librarians to cancel subscriptions to little-
used or unused periodicals is going to decline sharply.
The result is likely to be a great many cancelled subscriptions.
  Now I can hear the publishers muttering, "The librarians are entering into a conspiracy to put us out of
business." Nonsense. Librarians are simply going to stop
letting themselves be exploited. You don't think they
have been exploited? Here is another quote, which you
will also find in De Gennaro's *American Libraries* article. According to Baumol and Ordover, respected econo-
mists both:

> The fact is that a growing proportion of scientific
> journals have virtually no individual subscribers,
> but are sold almost exclusively to libraries, and
> that a high proportion of those journals are rarely,
> if ever, requested by readers. This suggests that
> many journals provide services primarily not to
> readers, but to the authors of the articles, for whom
> publication brings professional certification, career
> advancement and personal gratification.

  Now, if library budgets, which are supposed to be
used to provide services to their users, are, in fact,
providing a service to authors by purchasing subscriptions, is this not exploitation?
  Still another point. If the libraries have no voice
in the creation of new journals - and they don't - why

should the burden of preserving the channels of scholarly communication *in their present form* be forced upon them? Why should they bear the blame for the demise of endeavors which are not serving their users? Obviously, they shouldn't.

Now it is the authors who are muttering, "If a lot of these journals go out of business, there won't be enough to get all our papers published, or it will take years. You will be slowing down the growth of knowledge." Again, I say nonsense! In the first place, I suspect that the pressure of the "publish or perish syndrome" is great enough to force the creation of new channels and media for publication and communication, which is what the authors and publishers should be doing anyway.

Perhaps, we will be treated to a new *Journal of Inconsequential Research* totally paid for by page charges levied upon the authors and delivered free and preprocessed to libraries, provided only that they keep it on the shelf at least until the next issue appears.

While I may have appeared to be digressing, I have really been laying the groundwork for what comes next. It seems to me that overall impact of the new copyright law, taking into account all factors, will be to accelerate the development of networks and the national program. As the budget squeeze continues, and there is little reason to believe it won't, libraries are going to have to shift their emphasis more and more to acquiring that material which will satisfy most of the immediate needs of most of their particular clientele. This will mean foregoing the acquisition of little-used material, and relying on interlibrary loan for occasional uses, when it is cost effective. That is an important qualification, because interlibrary loan is not free, even if the lending library doesn't charge for providing the copy. With more and more libraries dropping marginal subscriptions, there will be a small but measurable increase in interlibrary loan traffic, as occasional-use material which was formerly available in-house now has to be obtained elsewhere. The increased recognition of dependence on other libraries will encourage libraries to join existing networks and consortia or form new ones. This will also hasten the development of union lists

and catalogs, which hopefully will promote the standard-
ization necessary for a national network. The increased
communications will increase the pressure for more effective and more economical telecommunications for library applications. The need for better information on
what they are doing will encourage libraries to keep
more complete statistics, which could, in turn, lead to
more widespread use of minicomputers, which could then
provide the capability for more effective management
tools and open the door for better use of new technology
as it develops. The ramifications are almost endless,
and all of them point in the direction of more cooperation, better communication, and more efficient use of
funds to provide better service - and that is what the
national program is all about.

Now I am not really as sanguine about the immediate
future as the foregoing may sound. As long as there is
uncertainty, and there will be for some time, some people and organizations are going to apply the most con-
servative interpretation in order to protect themselves
from any shadow of criticism. They will either quit photocopying altogether or else surround it with so many
protectionist requirements that ordering a photocopy
will become as difficult as correcting a billing error
in a computerized accounting system. Still others will
decide that it is all too complicated and that the record keeping is too much trouble, so they will also re-
treat into their shells. Such attempts to return to the
status quo ante bellum would be shortsighted to the
point of stupidity. We cannot go back; we must adjust
to the new situation and go forward, whatever the obsta-
cles and whatever the risks. Those of us who are committed to this must do our best to persuade others to follow suit.

For those of you who are afraid of being sued by
somebody for making copies of six articles from the
Journal of Endocrinic Chemistry, I think I can offer
some reassurance. In the first place, judging by the
Williams and Wilkins case, such a lawsuit is going to
cost the publisher several million dollars to prosecute,
so it will not be undertaken lightly. Ask yourself what
a publisher who is going to sue for infringement wants
to accomplish. In the first place, he wants to stop ex-

cessive photocopying of his journals or whatever. In the second place, and very, very important, he wants to collect damages, at least in an amount sufficient to cover the cost of the suit. Finally, he wants to have a very good chance of winning, so he will pick a big target and one he feels can be shown to be in blatant violation.

The next question to ask is which provision of the law he is going to sue under. The "six or more copies" of the guidelines? Not likely. Even if a librarian is so careless as to order that sixth article from some journal, it is highly improbable that this would happen often enough in a single institution to constitute blatant violation. No, if a lawsuit is filed, it will be on the basis of some other provision. Personally, I think it will be based on the "systematic" or "related or concerted" provisions of 108 g.

Therefore, the likely target is an institution which has a high volume of photocopying. How about the large research libraries, the Harvards, the Yales, and the Princetons? They are big enough, but they will only be doing what they have been doing for decades, so they are a part of "present practice," and they borrow heavily, even though they lend far more than they borrow. Perhaps the statewide networks, the NYSILLs, MINITEXes, and ILL NETs? No, they are distributive networks, with perhaps a central switching center for requests, but with fulfillment scattered all over the state. Maybe he will try a big urban library system that is making copies for its branches. Again, not likely. Considering the financial problems of urban libraries, and the cities themselves, for that matter, they can't be considered fruitful targets for a lawsuit.

Where, then, can the litigation-minded publisher find a large, "systematic," affluent (or backed by affluence) target? Well, there is NLM. They are a large, central source, and the ultimate resource of the regional medical library program. They are certainly a possibility, but they have been around a long time, and even under the new law, it is terribly difficult to generate much judicial outrage at an outfit which is trying to improve the practice of medicine, as Williams & Wilkins found out. Maybe the Center for Research Libraries (CRL) would make a good target? No, they too have been around a long time. Besides, their photocopying volume is not all that large. Most of their collection is monographs, which they lend in the original, and most of their journal article traffic is referrals to the British Library Lending Division. Maybe they can be nailed under Section 602, infringing importation? Again, that is a possibility, but who is going to be sued? I don't know what the figures are, but I suspect that most of those imported articles are foreign journals, and a foreign publisher would be at a disadvantage. Also, Section 602 refers to "no more than five copies" of a work. Even assuming that the article (rather than the issue) is the work, that is five copies of *each*, so CRL probably is not a good target.

The only real prospect the litigating publisher has left is the proposed comprehensive center of the periodicals access program. That program cannot wrap itself in the cloak of precedent; it will be a central source with high volume, and so on. So the center is sued. What then? Well, I honestly don't think the publisher would win, for the reasons I mentioned earlier, but let's assume the worst and suppose that the court rules for the publisher. Is this going to shut off interlibrary loan or even close down the center? Of course not! All it would mean is that the center would have to start paying royalties to the copyright holders, so the cost of operation and the cost of borrowing from it would go up. That certainly wouldn't be good. It would be bad and unjust, from the librarian's viewpoint. But it would not be the end of the world. The flow of information and our progress toward our stated ideal might be slowed a bit, but neither would come to a complete halt.

It all boils down to the fact that this country, the world, is rapidly becoming an information society. More and more, information is becoming necessary for survival and progress, and a national network of library and information services is essential for effective use of our information resources. The new copyright law may create some temporary dislocations, but in the long run, the net effect will be positive and hasten, rather than hinder, progress toward our ideal:

To eventually provide every individual in the United

States with equal opportunity of access to that
part of the total information resource which will
satisfy the individual's educational, working, cultural and leisure-time needs and interests, regardless of the individual's location, social or physical condition or level of intellectual achievement.

Association of American Publishers, Inc.

One Park Avenue
New York, N.Y. 10016
Telephone 212 689-8920

PROGRAM TO EXPEDITE THE PROVISION OF COPIES OF TECHNICAL-SCIENTIFIC-MEDICAL AND OTHER JOURNAL ARTICLES AND SHORT WORKS, AND TO EXPEDITE RELATED INFORMATION-SERVICE COPYING

*Prepared by the ASSOCIATION OF AMERICAN PUBLISHERS
TSM Copyright Clearance Center Task Force*

This program has been developed to help users to obtain copies of the journal articles and other short works needed to supplement their subscriptions but which are not available to them under fair use and related copyright provisions. It has also been designed to help to promote vital journal-publishing continuity. While the initial system places emphasis on articles in TSM (technical-scientific-medical) journals, because of the strength of demands in this area and the orientation of those involved in planning this program, efforts are already underway to expand the program to other short documents.

I. PUBLISHER PROCEDURES

1. *Initiation of the Program*

   Individual publishers of journals, magazines, and other collections of short works desiring to use the system will indicate their participation in this program by appropriately publishing on the first page of each article or short work (hereinafter referred to as "article") for which they require a copying fee a standardized code* that both identifies the article (and hence the publisher) and states the specific-

   ---
   * See Section I, Subsection 4.

article copying fee. Where participating publishers also require payment of copying fees for in-copyright articles that predate this coding, they will follow the listing procedure described in the next section.

2. *Establishment of a Copyright Clearance Center (CCC)*

As many as possible interested authors and publishers both for-profit and not-for-profit, will immediately join on a voluntary basis in the chartering, implementation, staffing, and operation of a not-for-profit copyright clearance center (CCC), to collect the fees for the copying of copyrighted journal articles which each publisher individually sets and prints on the first page of his journal articles. The CCC will distribute these fees (less a charge for processing) to the specific journal publishers identified in the stated-on-the-article codes. It is intended that these activities be operational by the target date of January 1, 1978, subject to any antitrust clearance which it may be appropriate to obtain.

The CCC will also collect and distribute pre-system copying fees for the copying of copyrighted journal articles published prior to January 1, 1978, when the specific participating journal publisher has recorded his journal title, ISSN, and pre-system fees with it in a manner that permits CCC-publication and distribution to users of appropriate lists of journal titles and their pre-system fees.

Publishers and authors will be among those represented on the board of directors of the CCC.

3. *Direct Licensing or Establishing of Print Centers*

Participating publishers retain the right to license other organizations to sell and quickly provide separates of articles. Others without a license may prepare such copies (not for public distribution) by paying the stated-on-the-article or listed fees through the CCC.

If it is discovered that other organizations do not successfully meet user demands for copies, the possibility of establishing cooperative print-supply centers or other supply mechanisms could be explored, provided any necessary antitrust protection would be available for the cooperative effort. Again, under such a system each publisher would establish his own individual pricing.

4. *Codes and Other Standards*

Wherever appropriate, the codes, journal titles and abbreviations, and other indicia established in ANSI/Z39 standards will be used in this system, or employed as developed. Assistance will be rendered ANSI/Z39 where feasible.

For use in this system, an article-identification code will immediately be established (preferably that being specified by ANSI/Z39, Subcommittee 34, if it is immediately available), one that will permit computer identification by the CCC of the specific publisher and also provision by the CCC to the publishers not only of payments, but also (on demand) identification of the specific articles copied and the individual numbers of such copies. This code will also require a direct statement in U.S. currency of the fee required for copying; at least this fee must be eye-readable, although the full code may eventually become machine-readable. These codes must appear clearly on all CCC-reporting copies as well as on all copies distributed to users. (It will be advantageous both to publishers and libraries if these codes are accompanied on the article and all copies by the copyright notice.)

It is contemplated that the Copyright Clearance Center will have the capability of distributing payments directly to authors when appropriate agreements so provide.

5. *Copying Fees*

Each individual publisher will set his own individual article-copying fees (if any). The publisher of each

journal will retain the right to establish whether
or not a given article or other journal document
(news story, "Note," editorial, etc.) will or will
not carry a copying fee, and what any fee will be.

6. *Fair Use and Sect. 108 d/g Copying*

TSM and other publishers will attempt to establish
voluntary guidelines jointly with authors and librar
associations for the fair-use and Sect. 108 d/g copy
ing that will not require the payment of fees. Pend-
ing the development of such voluntary guidelines, pu
lishers interested in the CCC-based program have gen
ally indicated that they will accept as Sect. 108 d/
copying *for participating-user organizations* either
the on-site making or the requesting from another li
brary, or both combined, of the number of copies (an
under the record-keeping and other conditions) spell
out in the CONTU guidelines for "Photocopying - Inte
library Arrangements."

7. *Universality of the System*

Congress will be urged to consider an appropriate um
brella statute as an amendment to Section 108 of the
copyright law, such that reasonable copying (not for
public distribution) could be undertaken of TSM arti
cles published after December 31, 1977, that do not
bear the code, subject only to the right of the non-
participating TSM journal publisher to collect a rea
sonable copying fee.

To assist users and to promote the growth of this
system, the CCC will publish before the end of 1977
a list of the publishers and their journals who are
participating or have so far indicated that they wil
participate in this program, and it will publish add
tional lists as appropriate.

The participation of foreign publishers publishing
journals abroad is being given special consideration
Reciprocal arrangements may need to be negotiated
with corresponding foreign payments centers.

Because demands exist and will grow for the provisio

of separates of other copyrighted short documents, such as items in other scholarly, general interest, business, and trade periodicals, the publishers of any or all of these can immediately participate in the current program by placing the proper codes on the first pages of their documents.

II. USER-ORGANIZATION PROCEDURES

1. *User-Organization Registration*

Copy-user organizations desiring to participate in the CCC program will be asked to register their intent to participate, their billing adress(es), etc., with the Copyright Clearance Center (CCC), in order to facilitate payments. The CCC will then issue to such participating-user organizations their appropriate organizational code or codes, preferably those established in or being developed by appropriate ANSI/Z39 subcommittees. (Failure to register will not exempt organizations from legal obligations to pay copyright owners in some manner.)

2. *Reporting and Paying for Copying*

Alternate mechanisms will be established for reporting and paying for CCC-based copying. The following, among others, seem to have merit, although it may not be possible to provide all of them.

a. User organizations not wishing to employ computerized-transactions reporting may make and send to the CCC a photocopy of the first page of each article photocopied or obtained for which payment is required.* The user will be required to mark each of these reporting pages with his appropriate organizational-copier code, and the number of copies made (e.g., "10 copies") when more than one is made. He will also be required to check reporting

---

*Plus for fair-use and related copies if studies in progress prove this to be mutually advantageous. (See also footnote in Section II, Subsection 2c.)

pages for pre-1978 articles to see that they bear
at least the title of the journal, the issue date,
and the initial page number of the article; if
not, he must write in the missing data. Bundles of
these reporting pages would be sent to the CCC at
least monthly.

b. User organizations wishing to employ computerized-
transactions reporting would periodically (at
least monthly) send to the CCC an appropriately
prepared computerized record of the article code
and copying price for each TSM or other coded article copied or obtained for which payment is required,* along with the number of copies made of
each such article if more than one. The CCC will
supply specifications for this reporting, and on
how to report copying of pre-1978 (uncoded) articles.

c. User organizations reporting their copying by
sending in a reporting copy of the first page of
each article copied or obtained may avoid any internal necessity for keeping records against later
billings by (if they are made available) using
stamping meters (leased through the CCC or otherwise obtained) to print the coded price (or aggregate for multiple copies) on the reporting copy.**
Alternatively, a participating user may buy from
the CCC or a designated agency adhesive stamps (if
they are made available) in appropriate denomina-
tions for affixing to each reporting copy. Prepayment may also be made by accompanying each collection of reporting copies with a corresponding
adding-machine tape and payment check.

---

*Plus for fair-use and related copies if studies in
progress prove this to be mutually advantageous. (See
also footnote to Section II, Subsection 2c.)

**If studies in progress prove it to be mutually advan-
tageous, user organizations will also be asked to report
fair-use and related copying; these reporting copies coul
be marked or stamped $0.00.

3. *Other User Requirements*

   a. All separates of articles must be reproduced exactly as published, with no textual or data alterations of any kind except for addition or notation of published errata. Addition of a copyright notice or system codes is permissible, of course.

   b. The CCC will not have authority to authorize users to produce copies for public distribution, e.g., for advertising or promotion purposes, for creating new collective works, or for resale to the general public as opposed to providing copies for internal use or for specific clients. Permissions for public-distribution copying should be obtained directly from the copyright owner.

   c. User organizations not employing a prepayment alternative should establish deposit accounts against which monthly charges would be reported and made. Monthly billings could be a further alternative, at least initially.

   d. If a participating-user organization is not a public, educational, or similar "public-type" library and wishes to authorize its non-library staff to make copies of copyrighted articles on unattended machines, it will be expected to inform these employees as to regulations and on how to indicate such copying, and it will be expected to devise effective ways to collect and to report this copying information to the CCC in order to pay for it. The CCC will supply appropriate phraseology for instructional posting at such copying-authorized unattended machines.

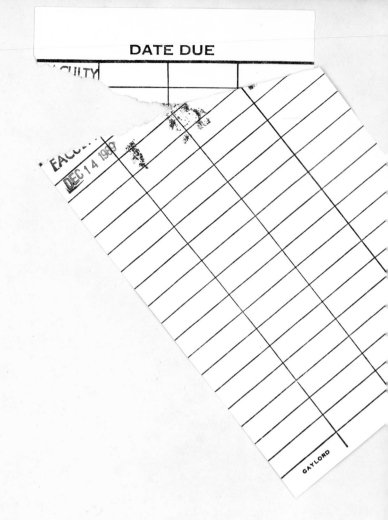